Images of War

GREAT WAR FIGHTER ACES 1914-1916

Norman Franks

Pen & Sword
AVIATION

First published in Great Britain in 2014 by
Pen & Sword Aviation
an imprint of
Pen & Sword Books Ltd,
47 Church Street,
Barnsley,
South Yorkshire,
S70 2AS

A CIP record for this book is available from the British Library.

ISBN 978 1 78383 182 1

Pen & Sword Books Ltd incorporates the Imprints of
Pen & Sword Aviation, Pen & Sword Maritime,
Pen & Sword Military, Wharncliffe Local History, Pen & Sword Select,
Pen & Sword Military Classics and Leo Cooper.

For a complete list of Pen & Sword titles please contact
Pen & Sword Books Limited
47 Church Street, Barnsley, South Yorkshire, S70 2AS, England

E-mail: enquiries@pen-and-sword.co.uk
Website: www.pen-and-sword.co.uk

Contents

Introduction   5

Chapter 1 – The First Air War   7

Chapter 2 – Things Get Serious   26

Chapter 3 – The Fokker's Day   47

Chapter 4 – Fokker Aces Supreme   61

Chapter 5 – Knights of the Air   81

Chapter 6 – Nieuport Scouts   101

Chapter 7 – Autumn Chill   115

Chapter 8 – The End of 1916   133

Introduction

This book looks at the development of air fighting on the Western Front in the Great War and the pilots who fought it, from its first tentative beginnings to the emergence of the fighter 'aces'. Everything was new and untried. It was up to the airmen of the day to gain experience, develop tactics and try to survive, in flimsy aeroplanes and with no parachutes.

Photographs

Having studied the air wars of 1914-19 and 1939-1945 for over fifty years, and having been a full-time military aviation historian for the last twenty-five, collecting images of the men and machines of both conflicts has not been difficult. Fortunately I was able to meet and correspond with a number of Great War veterans and almost all had their own collections of pictures, either taken by them or by friends who gladly had copies made for them and other men in their squadrons. I have been fortunate too to have been in contact with many brother Great War enthusiasts and, over the years, we have tended to copy and swap between us some of the more interesting photographs. Sadly a number of them have long since left the ground for the last time. However, I wish to thank those who have been pleased to help with photographs over the years: Greg van Wyngarden, Andy Thomas, Jon Guttman, Trevor Henshaw, Phil Jarrett, Stuart Leslie, Tony Mellor-Ellis, Walter Pieters, Andy Saunders, the late Mike O'Connor, Chaz Bowyer, Frank Cheesman, Ed Ferko, Neil O'Connor, Frank 'Bill' Bailey, Les Rogers and Hal Giblin.

Chapter 1
The First Air War

Nobody could have imagined what the bullets that hit and killed Austria's Archduke Franz Ferdinand, heir to the Austro-Hungarian throne, and his wife Sophie, on 28 June 1914, would lead to over the next four years. It triggered what became known as the First World War and, before it ended in November 1918, it had embroiled the United Kingdom, France, Germany, Belgium, Russia, Italy, the Austro-Hungarian Empire, Turkey, several Middle Eastern countries, the United States of America, and even Japan and China. On 28 July Austria and Hungary declared war on Serbia; Germany declared war on Russia on 1 August and, having demanded the right to advance through Belgium, then invaded France. Wanting to defend Belgium's neutrality, Britain declared war on Germany on 4 August.

In the past, major conflicts generally saw armies facing each other before one or the other moved forward, presaged by artillery fire and supported by cavalry. A battle won or lost usually meant that further battles would take place once each side had reformed and only after a number of engagements would one side surrender.

Although this new war, also referred to as the Great War, started out similarly, with France and Belgium under assault from Germany, and Britain going to their aid, the first fights were very much like the old days, although following the British Expeditionary Force's retreat from Mons, Belgium, it became obvious that Paris was soon going to be under threat. Further skirmishes slowed down Germany's push in that direction and then autumn gave way to winter. Few armies fought major battles in winter and, in many cases, the soldiers went home to await the spring. This time, however, rather than disperse each warring side 'dug in', that is to say, they dug massive trench systems that eventually stretched from the North Sea coast along what remained of unoccupied Belgium, right down to the Swiss border. Over the coming months these trench systems were enlarged and improved. They were not just a single long trench, but a massive series of trenches, those that were the front line, those deemed support trenches, plus a myriad of communication trenches that made the movement of men and supplies less vulnerable to fire from the opposition's trenches.

There were two things that followed which made the Great War in France very different. One was the wholesale setting up of massed barbed-wire entanglements, used to prevent enemy soldiers simply moving to occupy the opposing trench positions, and the other was the machine gun. Germany, France and Britain had developed the machine gun in the latter years of the nineteenth century, and these deadly guns were able to spit out streams of lethal bullets at men and horses if they were in the open. Thus, over the winter of 1914-15, little movement was made on either side. The men in the trenches kept a wary eye on the enemy trench systems, often only a few metres away, making sure they did not expose themselves to sniper fire, and hoping that the occasional artillery shell would not land in their trench, but explode either in front or behind.

One other problem with this new type of warfare was that the commanders, the generals and their staff officers, had almost no intelligence to help them plan an offensive so as to overcome this stalemate. In previous wars, it was the cavalry that rode across the countryside, to reconnoitre the 'other side of the hill'. The trenches and the attendant barbed wire made cavalry virtually obsolete overnight. However, there was a new concept in being – the aeroplane.

Aeroplanes had only been in existence for a few years and were far from reliable, and very flimsy in the extreme. However, those who supported the aeroplane had pressed their various cases, so much so that by 1912 the Royal Flying Corps (RFC) had been formed and even the Royal Navy had its air wing, which became the Royal Naval Air Service (RNAS) in mid-1914. Aeroplanes were, of course, few in number and even early units often had very differing types. However, the RFC had gone to war in August 1914 and a handful of squadrons was based on French soil. Meantime, the RNAS was mostly responsible for reconnaissance over the North Sea, looking for German shipping.

The generals, while reluctantly accepting that men in aeroplanes could fly over the lines, had little faith in what the airmen could see, some envisaging that the ground must look little more than a blur. They had no concept that, at height, much of interest could be seen. Once the intelligence began to be accepted the aeroplane suddenly had a place in war. One significant event that helped to change 'higher authority's' view was when Lieutenant L.A. Strange reported seeing strange streams of yellowish-green smoke coming from the German trenches on 22 April 1915. This was the first gas attack of the war.

By this time it was a daily event for aircraft of both sides to spy on what was happening behind the trenches, and the pilots and observers quickly began to recognise signs that could be read, determining what the opposition was doing. Of course, despite the very few aeroplanes about, it soon became obvious that Allied and German aircraft would meet, either going to or returning from a reconnaissance mission. It was only a small leap to realise that, quite apart from the 'sport' of engaging the other aeroplane, it was very much in each side's interest to stop the opposing crews from snooping about; thus the first hostile encounters ensued. Not that either side had much in the way of armament to engage the enemy. Aircraft were so light and flimsy that to attempt to carry any sort of armament and ammunition could seriously affect flight. One early enterprising pilot, Lieutenant Louis Strange (the man who spotted the first gas attack referred to above), having started flying before the war, found himself with No.5 Squadron RFC. Even before going over to France he had managed to attach a machine gun to his BE2c so that his observer in the front cockpit could engage an enemy. However, when he first encountered a German machine, he was unable to close with it, and upon his return his CO rebuked him, saying he had a better chance of catching an opponent if he didn't have the weight of this gun slowing him down. For a while afterwards he was only allowed to arm the aircraft with a rifle.

During the next weeks each side began to encounter the opposition. Some might try to fire a few rounds in the general direction of the other aircraft, but it was very hit and miss. After all, both were moving targets and had to contend with their aeroplanes' slipstream. The French too had their encounters, very much like their British allies. As the war began to settle down to a long stalemate on the Western Front, the British occupied the northern end of the lines from Belgium down to around Albert while the French held the line from there to Switzerland. It has to be remembered that, in the beginning, aviators of both sides were not divided into those given separate tasks but were 'maids of all work', each liable to be called upon to carry out a specific task. Only with time and experience did the air fighters emerge which led to scout squadrons being formed, differing distinctly from corps squadrons.

The German Air Service also had a variety of aeroplanes, mostly two-seaters whose role was that of aerial reconnaissance. Their crews, too, began taking guns up with them in case of the chance of an encounter. One major difference in the make-up of crews on either side was that with the British the pilot was in command; his observer, even if of higher rank, was subordinate to him. With the Germans, the observer was the man in charge, the pilot merely the 'driver'. Invariably the observer was an officer, the pilot an NCO. There were also varying types of individuals on both sides. Many pilots and observers were content to try and do their job of reconnoitring while others took a more offensive stance and were more than willing to take on any opposition they encountered. While this might be commended in certain circles, if they had a specific job to do – trying to locate a gun battery, or to confirm some enemy troop movements – going off for a scrap was not perhaps the most sensible thing to do. Nor did they want to over-tax their engines. To do their work of reconnaissance they had to fly over the enemy side of the lines and, while aircraft were able to glide some distance if their engines failed, it was not always certain they could make it. As the prevailing wind was generally west to east, the Allied airmen had also to contend with varying degrees of wind strength, something that might well hinder their progress home.

The first German aircraft shot down by the Allies was an Aviatik two-seater of *Feldflieger-Abteilung (FFA) 18,* on 5 October, flown by Sergeant Wilhelm Schlichting with Oberleutnant Fritz von Zangen, both of whom were killed. Their victors were Sergent Joseph Frantz and observer Sapeur Louis Quénault of Escadrille V24, the 'V' denoting that their unit used a Voisin two-seat pusher machine (the Voisin 3LA). Louis Strange and his observer Freddie Small brought down an Aviatik two-seater on 22 November 1914, on the Allied side. Strange later related that once the officer observer discovered his NCO pilot was unwounded, he began to beat and kick the man until British troops pulled him away.

What is meant by a 'pusher'? Despite the aeroplane being a new thing, there were any number of far-thinking men who were able to predict problems in the air, especially in a wartime scenario, but it didn't need a genius to realise that if an aircraft was being used to reconnoitre the ground a clear view forwards would not go amiss. Equally, those who also thought that if encounters with the opposition developed, a good view forwards would also be useful. The problem that needed to be overcome was how to get rid of the propeller which dominated the front of the aeroplane. The simple solution was to remove it and place it behind the aeroplane, so that, rather than pull the craft, it would push it! The 'pullers' were known as tractor engined.

France, Germany and Britain had worked this out before the war and each side had started to develop the concept. In France the Farman Company had built machines with engines behind, as had Caudron and Bréguet. Germany had the AGO C-types, and, later, some of their huge bombers had rear-facing engines. In Britain the Vickers Company had come up with the pusher idea as early as 1912, producing the Vickers FB5, while the Royal Aircraft Factory at Farnborough had also progressed with their FE2b two-seat machine and were planning a single-seat FE8. Geoffrey de Havilland was designing his DH2 for Airco – the Aircraft Manufacturing Company – that would see action in 1915. As air fighting increased, it became necessary to use these concepts, but it was also necessary to try and overcome the problem of firing forwards despite the obstruction posed by a propeller.

Using the pusher concept meant that there was no rear fuselage to the aeroplane because of the propeller. In order to accommodate rudder and elevators, wooden or tubular booms were fixed mid-way along the wings of the machine, angled to meet at the tail. The pilot or crew in these types sat in a gondola, or bath tub, arrangement in the front. Although having the advantage of forward view and a good forward field of fire, there was a degree of vulnerability to attack from astern, where most attacks originated. The engine might give some protection to the crew up front, but it meant the engine itself was vulnerable to damage. The Germans called these pusher-types 'gitterrumpfs' meaning 'lattice-tailed'.

Not for the first time in the war necessity became the mother of invention. To fire blindly through the whirring arc of a propeller would see the vast majority of bullets pass through it, although it wouldn't take too many strikes to cause damage and put the pilot in jeopardy. With tractor engines already available in large quantities, some way needed to be found to circumvent the propeller. The two main ways were either to fire over it or by it. Placing a machine gun on the top wing solved the problem of firing over the propeller, and fixing a gun at an angle by the side of the cockpit, set to fire to pass the propeller, was the other. The latter was always going to prove problematical and was not used very much, but the top-wing idea proved sound.

Several different tractor biplane types managed to fix guns to the top wing of an aeroplane and a cable was designed so that the pilot could pull the trigger that was out of reach. These guns needed to be drum-fed, rather than belt-fed. The French Nieuport Scout became the most famous fighter type to use it and it was also made possible for the pilot to pull down the gun in order to replace an empty ammunition drum, then ratchet it back into place. However, no sooner had these concepts taken root than the obvious solution started to appear. Shoot through the propeller arc *without* hitting the propeller.

Before this became a reality, the more adventurous, or perhaps foolhardy, pilots had decided on placing metal deflector wedges on each of the propeller blades so that the few bullets that would hit it would be 'pinged' off into space. A couple of French single-seat pilots began doing this. One was Roland Garros. Eugéne Adrian Roland Georges Garros had been born at Saint Denis on 6 October 1888 and had learned to fly in 1910. With the coming of war he, and many other pre-war aviators, volunteered their services – and their personal aeroplanes – to the French Air Force. Garros, as a mere Soldat 2nd Classe, was assigned to Escadrille MS23 (MS indicating the unit flew Morane-Saulnier aircraft). By the end of 1914 he had risen to commissioned rank and had become known for his aggressive stance against Germany. Often in action, he quickly deduced that the best way of hurting the enemy was to attack aircraft by flying directly at them. He had fixed a machine gun to the front of his Morane, set to fire directly through the propeller arc. In order to protect the propeller he had his mechanic, Jules Hue, fit metal deflector plates to the blades, invented by Raymond Saulnier (as an early form of interrupter gear), so that most of his bullets could be directed to the enemy from his line of flight. In April 1915 he managed to down three German machines. Fellow aviator Adolphe Celestin Pégoud also adopted this method.

Pégoud was eight months younger than Garros and came from Montferrat. Unlike Garros he had joined the military when he became 18 years of age, serving with the Chasseurs d'Afrique and later with an artillery regiment. Released from service in early 1913, his interest already directed to aviation, he gained his pilot's licence that same year. The parachute was another new invention, although it was not used in aeroplanes for some years; Pégoud made a parachute descent from a balloon in August 1913, and became the first aviator to 'loop the loop' a month later. With the rank of *brigadier* (corporal) he was assigned to an escadrille defending Paris when war broke out. By September 1914 he was flying reconnaissance missions in two-seater Maurice Farman 'pushers' with MF25. He and his gunner engaged three German aeroplanes on 5 February 1915, causing one, a single-seater, to fall, before attacking two two-seaters, one falling and the other going down to land.

This is an appropriate time to mention 'victories'. Apart from interest in Great War flying that was engendered in the 1930s through pulp fiction writers and journalists only too willing to jump on this bandwagon, it was not until well after the Second World War that would-be historians rekindled the public's interest in the exploits of Great War aviators. In the Second World War victories achieved by airmen of all sides were claimed as destroyed, but where a definite conclusion could not be ascertained it was deemed a 'probable'. If an opponent's aircraft was thought to be only superficially damaged, then it was treated as just that – damaged. Therefore, a fighter pilot achieving six enemy aircraft destroyed, two more probably destroyed and two others damaged, would have his score noted as six. However, in the Great War, depending on the period of the war in which the pilot was operating, his final score might be quoted as either eight or ten.

This was because, on the British side, a probable was counted as a victory from about mid-1916 and, previous to that, the damaged aircraft might also be counted, making ten. In general, the British recorded probables as 'out of control' and an aircraft which was seen to go down and land in its own territory, a 'forced to land' victory. Hugh Trenchard, head of the Royal Flying Corps in the early years, had made it policy to be offensive and take the war to the enemy. Therefore, most offensive actions by RFC and, later, RNAS units, were flown on the German side of the lines. In an air battle at height, it was not always possible to see if an opponent that began falling towards the ground following an attack actually crashed, as it appeared to be doing. All too often the 'successful' pilot was still in action and it would be foolish to watch an opponent spin down. Or the spinning or diving aircraft would be lost to sight due to it blending in with the landscape, or into low cloud or even ground mist. If another pilot confirmed seeing his comrade's victim spin down in such a way as to believe it would have crashed, then an 'out of control' victory would be counted.

Of course, it goes without saying that for a pilot of either side, if he found himself in a position where his opponent was obviously getting the better of him, it was all too easy to kick his machine into a spin and head down. Once clear of the immediate danger, he would right his aircraft and fly home, a wiser man – but alive. On the other hand, if one found oneself equally in danger of being shot down, it was wiser, especially for a German flying over his own territory, to go down and land, hoping his antagonist would leave him be. The 'victor' however, would have no way of knowing if he had inflicted any hurt upon either the aeroplane, its pilot or crew. Those who made a landing to get away from the danger might well be totally unharmed, but equally either the pilot (or crew member) may have been fatally, or seriously, wounded. That would mean, if fatal, he was out of the war just as certainly as if he had crashed from height.

Before the air war became too serious there was still much chivalry between opposing airmen, and men of both sides were satisfied that they had bested an opponent and forced him to land. In a way this moral victory also achieved another kind of 'victory'. In the case of a two-seat reconnaissance machine, forcing it down to land had prevented the enemy crew from carrying out their assigned task, whether it be pure reconnaissance, artillery spotting or photographic work. This was really the *raison d'être,* to stop or curtail the enemy's ability to carry out his operations.

The French noted 'probables' in a pilot's overall score, but only counted confirmed destroyed claims as victories. British and French pilots could also share victories and, again, those people who were later required to note a pilot's record would give one 'victory' to each pilot involved, be it two, three or even four. So one German aircraft shot down, during which four pilots helped with its destruction, would be credited with one 'victory' each in squadron records. On the German side, however, there was no sharing, and if more than one pilot contested the result, the combat would be reviewed and someone would decide on who should receive the victory. If it was too close to call, it could even result in a coin toss to make the final judgement.

For the British, the 'out of control' claims were felt fair due to the fact that, as virtually all combats were fought over the enemy side of the lines, there was no obvious wreckage to inspect, or prisoners to be taken. So it was deemed unfair that just because wreckage was not obvious, this 'out of control' (probable) victory should be ignored. Often a squadron intelligence officer would telephone a front-line position – a regiment or even artillery post – to ask if anyone had seen an aircraft fall and crash in a given location. Sometimes they could confirm seeing such an event, which might lead to a victory credit being given.

German pilots had some advantage over confirmation of claims in that they usually found evidence of a crashed aeroplane. Even so, there could be controversy as already mentioned. It is far easier, therefore, to discover who brought down a particular Allied aeroplane, but far more difficult for British or French claims. Both sides, on paper, had strict rules but, as history has shown, there were far more claims than reported losses. It also became a problem for the Germans if a victim fell or landed on the Allied side. Once again, a telephone call to a front-line army unit might prove useful, otherwise the Germans reported a 'z.L.gzw.' (*zur Landung gezwungen*), forced to land on the Allied side. Sometimes these failed to attain confirmation, although there were some times that such a claim was included in a pilot's score of victories. Sometimes, these Allied machines were within range of German artillery that would shell the machine to destruction.

✳ ✳ ✳

Flying a Morane Type L on 1 April 1915, Roland Garros shot down a German Albatros two-seater over Westkapelle, the crew being taken prisoner. That same day another Frenchman, and future ace, Sergent (later Sous-lieutenant) Jean Navarre, flying a two-seat Morane with MS12, brought down, with the aid of his gunner, Lieutenant Robert, an Aviatik B north of Fismes, the crew also being captured. On the 13th, he and Soldat Girard as gunner claimed another Aviatik. Jean Marie Dominique Navarre, born in 1895, was also a pre-war pilot from 1911 and naturally was quickly accepted into French military aviation when war started. Flying a single-seater in October he would gain his third victory.

On 3 April Pégoud, still with MF25 but now flying a single-seater, downed his fourth and fifth enemy aeroplanes, both two-seaters. He had reached the magic figure of five victories, although it must be said that, at this early phase of the war, there was no official yardstick in order to become what was later known as an ace. Nevertheless, he can be acknowledged as the first French ace of the new air war. One has to remember that everything was new. Each flight was something new to experience; in each combat pilots of both sides learnt valuable lessons if they survived, and even if they were brought down and lived, the lesson was even more valuable for the next flight.

Another pilot in Garros's escadrille, Eugene Gilbert, was yet another pre-war aviator, who, at 21 years of age, had become a pilot in 1910. Initially with a balloon unit he later became a military pilot in 1912. For a short period he became well known as a pilot who set flying records but rejoined the Air Service as war began. Like Garros, he initially flew two-seater Moranes with MS23 and gained his first victory as early as 2 November 1914, claiming a German Taube monoplane, assisted by his gunner, Capitaine de Vergnette. Flying with Soldat Bayle on 18 November, this team engaged a DFW BI near Rheims. Bayle's carbine fire holed the German's radiator, killed the observer and wounded the pilot, forcing the latter to land inside French territory. Again with Soldat Bayle he was credited with a third victory on 17 December, this time a DFW two-seater, although it may have been an early LVG machine. Victory number four, an Aviatik, came on 10 January 1915, flying with Lieutenant de Puechredon, near Amiens.

Garros's luck finally ran out on 18 April. By this time he had scored a total of three confirmed victories and one probable. He had become well known over the front but on this day he was brought down by ground fire in a Type L and captured. Inspecting his machine, the Germans quickly noticed his device for firing through the propeller and the story goes that a young Dutch aircraft designer, working for Germany (he had been turned down by the British and the French), was shown the deflector plates and asked to emulate it for their own tractor machines. The man, Anthony Fokker, was impressed but quickly thought that there was little future in this sort of thing, and that the real answer was to invent something that could be fitted to an aeroplane that would stop the gun firing for the split seconds the muzzle was directly in front of the propeller. He and his engineering team came up with a viable mechanism, called an interrupter gear, and, as it so happened, Fokker had a suitable aircraft to fit it to, which he did.

His aeroplane was a tractor monoplane, the Fokker M5K, and Fokker adapted it to carry a machine gun and successfully had it tested. The time of the Fokker Eindecker had begun.

In 1909, just three years prior to the forming of the RFC, Louis Blériot became the first man to cross the English Channel in his monoplane. Several of the type were built and pressed into service when war came. These flimsy-looking craft were used for early reconnaissance flights as the RFC moved into France.

The Morane Type L was used by the RFC and the French Air Force, although unarmed except perhaps for a rifle or carbine. Note the large underwing roundel to ensure that friendly ground forces did not fire on them.

The French Voisin designers, like several others, got round the problem of not being able to fire through the whirling propeller by putting the engine behind the pilot – the pusher concept. Two Voisin units were with the French when war began and the type was still in service four years later. It was whilst flying a Voisin pusher that Frantz and Quénalt brought down the first confirmed German aeroplane on 5 October 1914.

The Caudron G3 was another French aeroplane and, although its engine was in front, it had a lattice tail design, having the two-man crew in a nacelle at the front. These machines were at the front as war began and a larger, twin-engined, Caudron G4 arrived in early 1915.

The aeroplane was used almost exclusively for reconnaissance at the beginning of the war. An early German type was the Taube (Dove), the design built by several German manufacturers, the name being a generalisation. This Taube was built by the Rumpler Company. The design came into being in 1910 and a number of these machines were in private hands, but were pressed into service by the Germans once war began. Although unarmed, it could carry a small bomb load.

Two-seat biplane reconnaissance machines used by the German Air Service were the main targets in early air fights for Allied airmen. This is an Albatros C and its observer in the rear cockpit had the use of a moveable machine gun.

The **DFW C** two-seater was another reconnaissance machine often encountered by Allied airmen. This, too, had a rear-facing machine gun. DFW, Albatros and LVG two-seaters, in various designs, operated throughout the Great War.

The **Vickers FB5** 'Gunbus' had been around since 1912, the company realising that a better forward view and field of fire for a machine gun would be essential should war come. This pusher saw much active service in France, both for reconnaissance and early air-fighting, where the gunner/observer in the front part of the nacelle had a good all-round view despite suffering the blast of cold air. Early aviators were well protected by scarves, helmets and gloves while exposed flesh was generally smeared with whale grease.

A Vickers fighter of 11 Squadron in its Bessoneaux hangar. Note the protective canvas cover on the Lewis gun. The fuel tank is situated behind the pilot's cockpit.

This Vickers FB5 is pictured on the airfield at Vert Galand in 1915. Its crew, of 11 Squadron RFC, is preparing to take off, the propeller whirring and the gunner ensuring his gun is fixed properly. The indication 'A.J.I.' indicates the gunner is Lieutenant Algernon J. Insall, whose brother, Gilbert Insall, also 11 Squadron, was awarded the VC later in 1915. No. 11 Squadron was the first RFC unit to take the FB5 into combat as a 'fighting squadron'.

A poor photograph which, nevertheless, shows four men of 11 Squadron in front of an FB5 in 1915. Gilbert Insall is on the left, while his brother A. J. Insall is third from the left. The other two are named as Second Lieutenant Powell and Second Lieutenant R. A. W. Hughes-Chamberlain (observer).

Another early air fighter with 11 Squadron was Captain L. W. B. Rees. In 1915 he showed much aggression in air fighting that led to the award of both the MC and, later, the VC. Lionel Rees's claims show how 'victories' were assessed in 1915, with one LVG destroyed, one Albatros C captured, and four other enemy machines recorded as 'driven down'. Most of his victories were scored with his observer, Flight Sergeant J. M. Hargreaves DCM. His VC action was whilst commanding 32 Squadron (DH2s) in 1916, sending down one enemy aircraft 'out of control' and a second forced to land.

A crashed Albatros two-seater. If seen to do so it would have been allowed as a 'destroyed' victory.

A Morane biplane used by both British and French units in the early months of the war. This picture was taken in 1917 whilst it was being used as a training machine at the Central Flying School.

Another German two-seater often encountered was the Aviatik C.I. It is true to say that Allied pilots were not always certain of the German types they engaged and the term Aviatik often covered all types of enemy two-seaters.

Another early two-seater was the Rumpler BI, unarmed except for the observer taking either a rifle or carbine up with him for an attempt at protection against hostile attack. Note the additional iron cross marking on the upper surface of the lower wing.

Frenchman Roland Garros seated in his Morane L. A well-known pre-war aviator, he immediately volunteered for front-line action when war began and his aggressive stance led to some early victories. He was captured on 18 April 1915 and, although he escaped and returned to France in 1918, sadly he died in combat on 5 October 1918.

Garros's Hotchkiss machine gun mounting on his Morane N, also showing the deflector plate on the propeller blade.

Chapter Two
Things Get Serious

The first half of 1915 saw an increase in aerial activity over the Western Front. By now it had become obvious that the war had not been over by Christmas as many predicted and that, by digging in across France, there was a serious likelihood that it was going to drag on for some time. The generals, whose task it was to plan offensives in order to break this deadlock, now desperately needed the information about what the Germans, on the other side of the lines, were doing. Were they building up men and supplies for an offensive, or, if their own offensive was being planned, what sort of defences had the enemy in place?

Meanwhile, two things had developed on the flying front. From the very early days it had been possible for aeroplanes to carry a camera which was capable of taking reasonable photographs of the ground. As these improved with better lenses, there was far more information to be gained from studying the prints than from a written or verbal report from an observer, using just the Mark I eyeball. Therefore there was even more incentive to engage and drive off aircraft whose crews might well be flying a photo-reconnaissance sortie behind the lines.

With the war having come to a standstill, artillery units had set up batteries in appropriate locations which could be called upon to support a foray towards the opposite trenches, engage an opposing gun battery if located, or generally shell something that looked of interest. Hitherto, forward observation posts had been the main means of determining how well the firing was going, or if the targets were being suitably hit. The trench systems stopped most of that. However, aircraft flying over the lines could watch the fall of shot, record the explosions and, by the use of Morse code communication, the crews could adjust the shooting. In addition a crew on a reconnaissance might well discover a target of interest, and order up a few shells on it. This started each side's fighting aeroplanes flying offensive patrols to stop both types of activities. As the war progressed more and more army men began to be recruited to fly as observers, especially those already experienced in artillery work and able to identify suitable targets, or who knew how to direct artillery fire.

Observation balloons had been around for a long time, long before the beginning of the Great War, but they were being used increasingly for observing movement across the lines and also for directing artillery fire. Tethered to the ground, they were heavily defended with guns on the ground and even aircraft patrolling nearby, but as the war progressed, these balloons became targets for aggressive pilots, although not all were keen to take them on.

With both sides now determined to use interrupter gears in their fighting aircraft, usually referred to by this time as 'scouts', Anthony Fokker had led the way with his company's device fitted to his Fokker Eindeckers. It set in motion a definite increase in engagements. However, having gained an advantage with this interrupter gear, needed to be kept a secret for as long as possible. Added to this there was not a mass of Eindeckers available and, while production might be increased, it would all take time. Because of this the Germans did not allow their fighting pilots to cross the lines into Allied territory in case they were forced down, whereupon their 'secret weapon' would be discovered, and no doubt emulated. In this way the Germans began a mostly defensive air war, which did not alter even when numbers of fighters of all types increased over the next couple of years. This suited Trenchard's doctrine of always taking the war to the enemy, and naturally the German fighter pilots welcomed the 'flies coming into their parlour'.

Just like the Allied aviators there were those perfectly happy flying two-seaters on reconnaissance, photographic missions, artillery spotting or bombing, which had now started in earnest, rather than go hurtling over the lines looking for trouble. By this stage each individual army corps, whether British, French or German, had aircraft assigned to do whatever that corps needed. On the German side, in order to give some degree of protection for their two-seater operations, one or two Fokker Eindeckers were assigned to each *Flieger-Abteilung* (flying section). Due to the dearth of Eindeckers in France, this only allowed small number of 'fighters' to be assigned to each *abteilung*.

Pilots to man these first Fokkers came from the two-seater units themselves, but there was no lack of volunteers. Those with a more aggressive tendency, sometimes having already displayed a keenness to engage the enemy, were equally keen to fly the new monoplanes fitted with a forward-firing machine gun. Initially they flew just protection missions with their two-seater brothers, but between times they managed to fly alone or in pairs in an attempt to engage Allied machines over the front. The army at the front would readily telephone back to the airfields which had Fokkers, advising them where and at what height Allied aircraft were operating, or crossing the lines as if to head for a target to bomb. This would send the single-seat 'hotshots' into the air. Speed was not the major factor, the early Fokker only able to achieve around 80mph (130km/h), but as most British two-seaters managed only about 60-70mph, advantage was on the German pilot's side.

Overall aircraft numbers in the early summer of 1915, on the British front, were only just over 100, and these of varying types, in the nine RFC squadrons in the field. This was improving all the time, and while there were several fighting types, it was not until mid-1915 that a dedicated squadron came equipped solely with a fighter type (11 Squadron with Vickers FB5s).

One German two-seater unit that became famous was FA62 which set up camp at Douai, flying LVG C-type machines. It also received two Fokker EI fighters, and two pilots immediately volunteered to fly them. One was Oswald Boelcke, the other Max Immelmann. Boelcke came from Giebichenstein, near Halle on the Salle, Saxony, born on 19 May 1891, whose father was a rector of a Lutheran School. Many young Germans took the military as a career path, and the young Oswald entered the Prussian Military Cadet Corps after his twentieth birthday. Stationed at Darmstadt, he was close to a flying field and the aeroplanes he saw captured his interest. It took him some time to be able to transfer into aviation but he achieved this goal in June 1914 and, after the war began, he and his brother Wilhelm were both flying with FA13 on the French part of the front over the Argonne. He was with this unit for seven months, being awarded the Iron Cross First and Second Class. He also flew the unarmed Fokker M5K, something that was to prove an advantage at Douai.

His first aerial combat took place on 4 July 1915, still flying a two-seater, his observer's fire bringing down a French Morane Parasol. To illustrate the often hit-and-miss nature of combat, his observer fired 380 bullets from his gun, and examination of the wreckage showed only twenty-seven had hit the target. However, both Frenchmen had been killed by some of the bullets, ending their flight that day.

Max Immelmann was also a Saxon, born in Dresden on 21 September 1890. In 1905 he too joined the military at the local cadet school. Soon after war was declared he also had become interested in aviation and applied for a transfer. Becoming a pilot he was firstly assigned to FA10 and then to FA62, where he became firm friends with Boelcke. At first, Immelmann began flying Boelcke's LVG once the latter had begun flying one of the Fokkers. On 1 August 1915, Boelcke was up after British aircraft, finding a formation of BE2 machines on a bomb raid (the contemporary term for a bombing raid) to a target near Douai. As the German attacked, so his gun jammed and reluctantly he had to break off. However, having also heard the news of the British incursion, Immelmann had jumped into the second Fokker and headed for the action, arriving just as Boelcke was turning away. He continued the attack and brought one of the BEs down for a forced landing, its wounded pilot being captured. With the chivalry that was evident in these early days, Immelmann flew an LVG across the lines the next day, dropping a message that his wounded victim was safe, although a prisoner.

This victory is believed to have been the first achieved by a Fokker pilot, although Leutnant Kurt Wintgens, flying a Fokker with FA67, might also have claimed the first. Born in 1894, Wintgens had also been an army cadet, and when war began saw action on the Eastern Front, winning the Iron Cross Second Class. Before the end of 1914 he had transferred to aviation and actually trained at the Fokker Flying School at Schwerin, so being sent to FA67, it was natural for him to be given one of its Fokkers. His first combat came on 1 July, shooting down a French Morane L, but as it appeared to come down inside French lines it remained unconfirmed. However, it did come down, with both crewmen wounded. Wintgens would have to wait for his first *official* victory. Of interest, Wintgens did not have the usual requirement of good eyesight, and actually wore spectacles, both on the ground and in the air.

Boelcke, Immelmann and Wintgens each scored victories during August 1915 and, by the end of the year, Boelcke was able to claim a total of six victories and Immelmann seven. Wintgens was not to add to his early tally until 1916, but three more emerging aces began to score in late 1915: Leutnants Otto Parschau, Gustav Leffers and Oberleutnant Ernst Freiherr von Althaus.

Parschau, who came from Klutnitz, East Prussia, was born on 11 November 1890 and was yet another pre-war soldier. Learning to fly in 1913 he had been sent to

FA261, flew a Fokker, but then went to a bombing unit, although he also flew Fokkers on escort duty with it. On 11 October 1915, flying over the Champagne area, he engaged a Farman and claimed it shot down. No French losses are recorded on this date, but one on the 12th seems to fit, so perhaps the date was wrongly recorded by one side or the other. On 19 December Parschau achieved his second victory over a British BE2c. More would follow in the new year.

Gustav Leffers hailed from Wilhelmshaven, in northern Germany, and was born on 2 January 1892. He had been studying engineering as war began and he immediately volunteered to become a pilot. Achieving this, he was assigned to FA32 in February 1915 to fly LVG two-seaters but, tiring of this, volunteered for Fokker training and on 5 November, completing the transfer, was ordered to fly a Fokker back to his unit. However, a problem during landing caused him to crash, writing off the Eindecker although he was not harmed.

Exactly one month later, on 5 December, he achieved his first kill in a Fokker, downing a BE2c whilst operating from Vélu airfield, north of Bertincourt. He was looking for reported British machines and exploding anti-aircraft fire alerted him to the enemy's position. He quickly despatched the British machine, which came froms13 Squadron. This Squadron lost a second BE this day, its victor being von Althaus. He had been born in March 1890 and was the son of the adjutant to the Duke of Saxe-Coburg-Gotha. He had joined the military in 1908, entering the 1st Saxon Hussar Regiment as a cornet. Commissioned in 1911 he saw action when war began, winning the Saxon Knight's Cross of the Order of St Heinrich in January 1915. He then moved to aviation.

Promoted to oberleutnant, he requested pilot training and, having achieved this, was posted to FA23 in September 1915, and was soon flying an Eindecker. He achieved his first victory on the same day as Leffers and there were some strange coincidences in the two events. Leffers shot down BE number 2049, while von Althaus' BE was 4092, the same numbers but in a different order, and both BE pilots were Australian. All four men, two pilots and two observers, lie together in Achiet-le-Grand (Extension) Cemetery. Once again a message was dropped over the British lines, informing the RFC of their fate.

Another future ace opened his account on 19 September 1915, this being Leutnant Hans-Joachim Buddecke. Born in Berlin in August 1890, he had joined the army in 1904 but left in 1913 in order to work in the United States, in his uncle's car factory. Whilst in the US he learnt to fly. With money presumably not being a major problem, he even purchased his own aeroplane, a French Nieuport. However, war ended all this and he returned to Germany and volunteered for the air service. He was assigned to FA23 and when a Fokker arrived in 1915 it was suggested he fly it, having flown a monoplane before the war. Buddecke began escorting the unit's AEG twin-engined machines, although it took some weeks before he had a successful action. He engaged a BE2c over the lines and shot it down, resulting in the award of the Saxon Knight's Cross of the Military St Henry Order. While not a Saxon himself, he had close association with Saxony. The citation for this award read:

> On 19 September 1915, Ltn. Buddecke set out on a Fokker fighter monoplane (single-seater) against an English plane which had forced another plane of his Section down after a short fight and was bombing the city of Cambrai. Ltn Buddecke got within ten metres of the English plane. During the combat he fired almost 700 rounds. The enemy plane received 109 hits and was forced to land behind our lines (pilot dead, observer captured). Only his extraordinary handling of his aircraft and personal courage allowed such a result against a comparably equipped enemy.

⁂ ⁂ ⁂

Across the lines on the British side, the RFC pilots were becoming no less aggressive than their German counterparts. Captain L. G. Hawker was a pilot flying with No. 6 Squadron equipped with Bristol C Scouts. Lanoe Hawker came from a distinguished military family, and was born in 1890. He joined the Royal Engineers and transferred to the RFC pre-war, having learned to fly privately at Hendon. He had gone to France in October 1914, his unit being equipped with Henry Farman machines, later converting to BE2c types. With a BE he took part in several missions, including a bomb raid upon Zeppelin sheds near Gontrude, for which he received the DSO. Somewhat like the German practice, with the arrival of some single-seat Bristols in mid-1915, some were assigned to the corps squadrons, and one, serial number 1611, was sent to 6 Squadron and taken over by Hawker.

The Bristol was a tractor-type aeroplane and, of course, the problem of firing to miss the propeller was uppermost in Hawker's mechanical mind. He got round it by fitting a Lewis gun on a support bracket by the port side of the cockpit, fixed to fire obliquely forward, therefore missing the propeller blades. He could operate the gun and could exchange an empty drum of ammunition for a full one, although obviously his attack approach was slightly crab-like. Nevertheless, he was an aggressive airman and, on 21 June 1915, forced a DFW down 'out of control' over Poelcapelle, Belgium. Four days later he attacked an Albatros two-seater that fell in flames to crash inside British lines. The German pilot died in the fiery crash, the observer having been flung out as his machine fell. For this action, Hawker received the Victoria Cross, the first ever VC awarded for air combat.

In August the Squadron had received some FE2b two-seat pusher aircraft, and flying these he achieved a further three victories, followed by a seventh in September back in a Bristol. He is considered to be the first British ace. Returning to England he later took command of 24 Squadron, of which we will read more later.

Like a number of pilots, Lieutenant E. L. Foot, known as 'Feet' to his comrades, began his flying career as an observer on two-seater Corps machines with 4 Squadron in the spring of 1915. He also knew what it was like to be shot down, having been brought down on 21 July, along with his pilot, but luckily they emerged unhurt from the wreckage and on the British side. He returned to England to train as a pilot, returning to serve with 11 Squadron, now equipped with a machine rather better than the old Vickers FB5, the FE2b.

The FE2b was a large machine, but not so unwieldy as to fall victim to nimble German Fokkers. It was another pusher-type built by the Royal Aircraft Factory, the FE standing for fighter experimental. It was born from the FE2a, a pre-war design to overcome the problem of firing forward in flight. The 2b began to arrive in France during mid-1915 and, on 9 September, Ernest Foot, with observer Second Lieutenant G. K. Welsford, fought two German two-seaters above Irles, claiming both as destroyed. On the 15th they destroyed a German scout. Promoted to flight commander, he was posted to 60 Squadron and, flying a Spad VII, on 28 September shot down an Albatros two-seater. In a Nieuport Scout on 21 October he sent a Roland CII down 'out of control'. These victories resulted in the award of the Military Cross.

Five days later he was himself shot down in flames in his Nieuport, the German pilot being Leutnant Hans Imelmann of Jasta 2, not to be confused with Max

Immelmann (note spelling), although both had flown together in FA62. Foot once again survived and was soon sent home to rest, and later helped form No. 56 Squadron.

Another British ace who, like Hawker, flew Bristol Scouts but with 10 Squadron, was a well-known pre-war airman, Charles Gordon Bell. From London, born in 1889, he learned to fly at Brooklands in 1910 and gained fame in pre-war aviation circles. By the time war began he had flown sixty-three different types of aeroplane, no mean feat at this early stage of flying. Joining the RFC in late 1914 he went to France and, like other early aces, immediately projected an aggressive attitude. Between 19 September and 30 November he claimed five German two-seaters, one destroyed, two 'out of control' and two forced to land. There is a suggestion that his score may have been higher as he had been engaged in numerous combats, but it took its toll and eventually he was forced to return to England due to ill health. He was later an instructor, one of his pupils being future top ace James McCudden VC DSO MC. Well known for his stammering speech, a monocle in one eye and a ready wit, Bell was killed in a flying accident in France in July 1918.

On the French front, one of the more colourful budding aces was the already mentioned Jean Navarre whose twin brother died in flight training. Although there is a record of him obtaining a civil flying licence in 1911, it is also suggested that he lied about this in order to gain entry into French military aviation. Whatever the truth, he certainly made his mark after he entered the military in 1914 and qualified for his military brevet in September. Initially posted to Escadrille MF8, he then went to MS12. He downed his first enemy machine – an Aviatik – on 1 April 1915, shared with his observer Lieutenant Robert followed by another Aviatik on the 13, along with Soldat Girard. By 23 October he was flying a single-seater Morane, and gained victory number three, an LVG. This machine came down in French lines, its pilot fatally wounded, the observer just wounded. For these early feats he received the Médaille Militaire and the Légion d'Honneur. We shall read more of his exploits in a future chapter.

Adolphe Pégoud, now wearing the Médaille Militaire and Croix de Guerre, had moved to Escadrille MS49. Commissioned, he continued to fly Moranes over the front, gaining his sixth official victory (plus three probables) over yet another Aviatik on 11 July 1915. However, he met his fate on 31 August. He engaged an Aviatik of FA48 on a photo-reconnaissance mission but was hit by fire from the German observer, Leutnant Bilitz, and fell to his death. Ironically, the pilot of the two-seater, Unteroffizier Kandulski, had been a former student of Pégoud.

Another well-known pilot in the early part of the war was Armand Pinsard. He also entered the military prior to the war, and served with the 2nd régiment de spahis algeriens in North Africa. He was twice decorated for heroism but moved to aviation in 1912 and was even decorated for his actions in army manoeuvres the following year. At the start of the war he was assigned to MS23, where he met Garros and others. He received two further citations but was forced down in enemy territory on 8 February 1915 and taken into captivity. Ordinarily this would have ended a career that had begun so successfully, but after fourteen months he and another well-known aviator, Capitaine Victor Ménard, managed to escape from their prison and, on 10 April 1916, crossed into safety. He would return to active duty and become a high-scoring ace, flying Nieuports and Spads during 1917 and 1918. Ménard would go on to command a fighter escadrille (N26) with Pinsard as one of his pilots. He later commanded a whole fighter *groupe*, and then an escadre de combat.

Edwards Pulpe was yet another to fly with MS23. Born in Latvia in 1880 he had become something of a traveller and, finding himself in France, learnt to fly in 1913. With the coming of war he offered his services to the French and by May 1915 was with MS23. In October he received the Médaille Militaire. Flying over the Verdun front he was credited with two victories, although full details have been lost, but he achieved ace status in 1916.

Eugene Gilbert had gained his fourth victory with MS23 on 10 January 1915, an Aviatik north of Amiens, with Lieutenant Puerchredon as his gunner. He was then posted to MS37, but when MS49 was formed in April he was sent to it. His fifth victory came on 7 June, and number six on 17 June, both whilst flying a single-seat Morane. Then his luck ran out, being forced down over the Swiss border on 27 June. Twice he got away from his prison camp, being recaptured during the first attempt but his second, on 5 June 1916, was successful and he scrambled back into France. Unable to fly further combat missions, he became a test pilot but was killed in a flying accident in May 1918. He had received the Légion d'Honneur, Médaille Militaire and Croix de Guerre with four *Palmes*.

Two future top aces had tentative beginnings in 1915, Georges Guynemer and Charles Nungesser. Georges Marie Ludovic Jules Guynemer became the darling of

France through his exploits in 1916-17 but, as a lowly *soldat* pilot in 1915, he was flying two-seat Morane reconnaissance machines. Born in Paris on Christmas Eve, 1894, he volunteered for active service in November 1914, and became an aeroplane mechanic. Despite being a rather sickly child, his determination to achieve his goal as a pilot was eventually met and he received his military brevet in April 1915, and in June went to MS3 as a caporal, then sergent in July, the day after he and his gunner, Soldat Guerger, brought down an Aviatik. This feat also brought him the Médaille Militaire.

Back on the British front, Gilbert Insall VC and his observer, Corporal T. H. Donald, engaged a German two-seater on 14 December 1915 but came off second best. Donald was wounded in the leg and Insall was hit in the back by a shell fragment, which led them to make a forced landing and be captured. The German crew consisted of Hauptmann Martin Zander and Leutnant Leche of FFA9. For Zander it was his third victory and he later became CO of Kek Nord. In 1917, as commander of Jasta 1, he would add three more kills to his tally.

'Kek' was short for *Kampfeinsitzerkommando* – meaning a group of one-seater fighting aircraft, mostly equipped with Fokkers. KekN meant Kek Nord (north), while KekV was for Kek Vaux, KekB for Kek Bertincourt, and so on. These were small groups of Fokker pilots grouped together to work in conjunction with the FA units, but were not specifically attached to them. Their name indicated the base from which they operated.

Anthony Fokker, the Dutch aircraft designer, who did much for the German Air Service in the First World War, providing them with several famous fighter aircraft. He is standing in front of his first success, the Fokker monoplane.

Anthony Fokker seated in one of his M5K machines, fitted with a machine gun set to fire through the propeller arc. Note that this early gun comes with a rifle-like stock. Note, too, the pilot's head-rest. The array of wires is for warping the wings before ailerons began to be used.

Kurt Wintgens seated in an unarmed Fokker A, probably at Schwerin when he was training. Note the petrol tank cap behind the cockpit and the cutaway wing root so that the pilot can see the ground easier, especially when landing. Wintgens is wearing glasses – pince-nez – that will be held in place when he lowers his goggles.

Willi Rosenstein of FA19 seated in a Fokker EI in August 1915. Between September and October he flew twenty-three front-line flights and had several combats, all of them proving inconclusive. He became a pilot in 1912, but when the war began he served in the army before transferring to aviation. He flew Fokkers and later flew as Hermann Göring's wingman in a jasta. He claimed nine victories during 1917-18.

Flieger Jakob Wolff was another Fokker pilot, this time with Kampstaffel Metz. This picture shows to good effect the wires to the wings, for the Fokker had no wing ailerons, lateral movement being achieved by warping the wings. Most early monoplanes had to adopt this method of flight control.

Lanoe Hawker VC DSO, the RFC's first ace, although the method of determining a pilot's score changed greatly as the war progressed.

Hawker's Bristol Scout (1611) clearly showing the angle that the gun was mounted at in order to miss the propeller arc.

Captain E. L. Foot as an observer in 4 Squadron in 1915, before becoming a pilot. In June 1916 he joined 11 Squadron on FE2b machines and, with his observer, claimed three victories resulting in the award of the **MC**. Before the end of the year he had flown with 60 Squadron and brought his score to five.

This is a superb picture of the FE2b showing the observer's two guns and the pilot's one fixed gun. A camera can be seen fixed to the port side of the nacelle. This is a 20 Squadron machine photographed in 1917, its crew being Captain F. D. Stevens and Lieutenant W. C. Cambray MC.

Captain C. G. Bell also became an ace, claiming at least five 'victories' between 19 September and 30 November 1915, flying Bristol Scouts with 10 Squadron. He is standing in front of a Blériot.

It was not all air-fighting. This BE2c (1680) was being flown in the early morning of 13 September 1915 on a spy-dropping mission. Unfortunately, the pilot, Captain T. W. Mulcahy-Morgan, originally commissioned in Princess Victoria's (Royal Irish Fusiliers), of 6 Squadron, hit a tree, was injured and taken prisoner. He managed to escape and returned to the UK in April 1917. Three days before his crash he had shot down a German Albatros while flying a Martinsyde S1.

Adolphe Pégoud who gained six
official victories in 1915 with MF25
before falling himself in combat with
MF49 on 31 August 1915. He is seated
in a Blériot monoplane.

Jean Navarre had three
victories in 1915 with MS12,
but his glory days would come
in 1916 with N67. He is
wearing the Légion d'Honneur,
awarded on 2 August 1915.

Georges Guynemer's crashed Nieuport 10 Scout. The picture is dated, and signed by Guynemer, 30 November 1915. His days of glory were still to come.

Georges Guynemer by his Nieuport Scout. He named all his aeroplanes 'Vieux Charles' (Old Charles). He is wearing the medals of the Légion d'Honneur, Médaille Militaire and Croix de Guerre with four *Palmes*.

Charles Nungesser scored his first victories in 1915, including one as a two-seat pilot. He ended the war with forty-two victories, having been awarded virtually every decoration that it was possible to win.

A BE2c of 8 Squadron RFC, brought down by Hans-Joachim Buddecke, for his first victory, on 19 September 1915, flying Fokkers with FA23.

Hans-Joachim Buddecke who would score many victories in the Middle East.

The first victory of Gustav Leffers on 5 December 1915. The BE2c came from 13 Squadron. Both crewmen died.

Yet another BE2c, this one from 12 Squadron, shot down by Otto Parschau of KG1 on 19 December 1915. This was Parchau's second victory. Both RFC men died and were buried by the Germans who used the empennage from their aeroplane to form a cross on the grave. The observer, Lieutenant D. F. Cunningham-Reid, had a brother Alec, who would become an ace with 85 Squadron in 1918.

The Morane Parasol of 3 Squadron, brought down by Max Immelmann on 15 December 1915 for his seventh victory. The crew were killed.

Chapter Three
The Fokker's Day

As 1916 began the Fokker Eindeckers had become dominant in the skies of France and would continue to be so for several months. More Fokkers were being built and some of the two-seater units were having their allocation of Eindeckers increased while the High Command were happy to see small groups of single-seaters operate independently to engage British and French aircraft flying over the front lines.

The Allied commanders were well aware of the dangers their airmen faced and had been desperately seeking aircraft that could match effectively, and hopefully defeat, what was fast becoming known as the 'Fokker Scourge'. The arrival of the French Nieuport Scouts was a step forward and, in February 1916, the first dedicated RFC single-seat fighter squadron arrived in France, again with a new type. This was No. 24 Squadron; its equipment was the de Havilland 2.

The DH2 was another pusher-type that was highly manoeuvrable; once its pilots had become familiar with it they would soon begin to regain some measure of air dominance over the Fokkers. A handful of DH2s had already been sent to France and, like the Germans, had been allocated to a few corps squadrons. A second DH2 unit, 29 Squadron, would arrive in France in March, and 32 Squadron would boost the DH2 presence in May. A not dissimilar looking aircraft, the FE8, was also close to production and 40 Squadron RFC would bring them to France in July 1916. Another new type that was about to be sent to 27 Squadron in early 1916, which took them to France on 1 March, was the Martinsyde G100 'Elephant'. Described as a scout and bombing aircraft, it was more proficient in the latter role. A Lewis gun mounted on the top wing provided forward fire, and later this was augmented by fitting a second Lewis gun on a spigot behind the cockpit on the port side. However, it could not possibly be aimed with any accuracy and so was more or less just a scatter gun to 'frighten' a pursuing German.

Some Fokker pilots were now mounting twin Spandau machine guns on their machines, firepower being deemed preferable to speed, as they had little difficulty in overhauling the slower Allied corps machines. There was also a new, similar, kid on the block, the Pfalz E monoplane. It looked so much like the Fokker that in the heat of combat no Allied pilot needed to bother about which type they were fighting, but the Pfalz was not as successful as its cousin and its operational life was short. They were later used mainly on the Eastern Front.

* * *

The Fokker pilots with FA62 continued to score over Allied machines in January 1916. Oswald Boelcke claimed three, to bring his score to nine, while his rival Max Immelmann got just one, to make his total eight. However, it was enough to bring the highest Prussian award to both men, the *Orden Pour le Mérite* (the Blue Max). These awards, the first to aviators, were both dated 12 January 1916, and the yardstick for such an award was stated as being eight confirmed victories in aerial combat. It was certainly a boost for the Fokker pilots on the Western Front, and it was not unusual for further decorations to follow. With Germany made up of several states, Prussia, Bavaria, Saxony, Württemberg, and the Duchies of Baden and Oldenburg, etc., it wasn't long before some of these states began to shower war heroes with their own, often highly colourful, awards and decorations. It must have been heady stuff for the recipients.

Two other Fokker pilots began to emerge in January, Wilhelm Frankl and Walter Höhndorf. Frankl came from Hamburg, born in December 1893, and had learned to fly in 1913. He started his war as an observer with FA40. He was decorated with the Iron Cross for downing an enemy machine with carbine fire on 10 May 1915 although this was never included in his overall score. It was not until he began flying Fokkers with Kek Vaux that he had confirmed victories, the first three being French Voisins in January and February 1916.

Walter Höhndorf, from Prutze, born in 1892, had become a pilot in Paris during 1912 and was a noted airman before the war. He was a test pilot during 1915 but then managed a posting to the front, joining FA12 as a Fokker pilot. He downed two French Voisin machines in January 1916, but then moved to Kek Vaux.

Buddecke downed his fourth on 6 January and his fifth on the 12th, but these were claimed against the RNAS in Greece, operating with the Turks, as he had been posted there to join FA6. In between these dates he had three disallowed claims. By the end of January he had raised his tally to seven. His next claim was another not confirmed, but nevertheless for his actions he became the third German fighter pilot to receive the *Pour le Mérite* on 14 April.

Immelmann and Boelcke both scored in March, with four and five victories respectively, bringing both men's totals to thirteen. Another pilot in FA62, Max von Mulzer, shot down his first British aeroplane on 30 March. At this stage there were four Fokker pilots with FA62 (now also known as Kek Douai), Boelcke, Immelmann, Ernst Hess and Albert Österreicher. Hess, from Wiesbaden, born in 1893, had also learned to fly in 1913 and was on two-seaters when war began. His first victory with the Fokker came on 5 January 1916, but it was his last for some months. His success began in 1917.

Otto Parschau added two more to his total in March, one being a French Nieuport Scout. His unit was now operating over the Verdun front. Defending the city of Verdun was a major effort for the French in 1916. Losing it was just not an option and battles raged about this city for most of the year. Some half a million men from both sides would die in the fighting. The French Air Service was in the thick of the defence although they were hardly capable of stemming the mass of German aircraft thrown into the offensive. Nieuport Scouts had now equipped several French fighter escadrilles and they were able to put up small patrols over the battle. Indeed, at one point they were ordered to keep aircraft in the air at all times. Escadrille N3, which would became one of the premier French fighting units, was in the thick of the action, but it was N65 that scored the most victories by mid-April, at which time the French regained air supremacy. Charles Nungesser had accounted for five in April, three two-seaters, one single-seater and one balloon.

Kite balloons were not only legitimate targets, and important ones, but their destruction counted in a pilot's personal tally. On the face of it they might seem easy targets, being a huge fat floating object full of inflammable helium, but they were far from that. Destroying them meant, of course, that the Germans were less able to observe what was going on, and it took a while for a replacement to be shipped in. Even compelling the winch crew to pull the balloon and its observer down helped. In the attacks it was most likely that the observer, being equipped with a parachute, would jump from his swinging basket. These parachutes were generally fitted to the outside of the basket with ropes attached to the observer; jumping out, his falling body weight pulled the stowed canopy from the pouch and, hopefully, the man would fall gently to the ground, provided the burning balloon mass did not envelop him on the way down.

Albert Louis Deullin, a former dragoon, transferred to aviation in April 1915 and was decorated as a reconnaissance pilot that summer, even being credited with a victory with his observer. Moving to N3 he too saw early combat over Verdun, raising his score to four by the end of April. Although wounded in combat on 2 April he was back in the air two weeks later. He received the Médaille Militaire and was made a Chevalier of the Légion d'Honneur. The latter came after bringing down a German machine over the front line, falling near the French trenches in full view of his countrymen. Guynemer had gained his eighth victory, and Chainat two. Andre Julian Chainat was 23 years old and a former artilleryman, but moved to aviation in 1914. He flew with two other Morane escadrilles before joining N3 and would become an ace by the summer.

We read earlier of Jean Navarre of MS12. In early 1916 he had transferred to N67 and made his name in the skies above Verdun. On 26 February he downed a Fokker EIII and a two-seater. Leutnant Alfons von Zeddlemann of KGI (Kasta 2) was escorting a two-seater of the same unit (Kasta 4). Zeddlemann was killed, while the pilot of the two-seater died of his injuries; his pilot, Oberleutnant Heinrich Kempf, was taken prisoner.

On 2 March Navarre downed an Albatros C, then claimed other enemy aircraft (EA) on the 19th, and on 3 and 24 April, bringing his score to nine. He flew a distinctively-marked Nieuport which was often seen in the air by ground troops, who began to refer to its pilot as the guardian of Verdun. In May he scored twice more and his final victory came on 17 June. However, he was badly wounded on this date and although he got down safely he had flown his last combat mission. He was killed in a flying accident in July 1919.

* *

On the British Front, Jack Armand Cunningham, a 25-year old Liverpudlian, was flying with 18 Squadron in 1915, forcing down an LVG in November in an FB5. On 29 December, flying a Bristol Scout, he added an Aviatik,. In early 1916 his squadron was one of those to receive a couple of DH2s for escort work and, on 5 February, Cunningham shot down an Albatros C-type. However, none of the three was confirmed as destroyed, but he would gain several of this type later in the war.

One pilot to overcome a Fokker monoplane was Second Lieutenant Lord Doune. Francis Douglas Stuart-Grey Doune, the eldest son of the 17th Earl of Moray, was born in July 1892. He became a founder member of 25 Squadron, with FE2b machines and, on 29 April 1916, he and his observer spotted a Fokker near la Bassée. Doune dived at it, closing to about sixty yards, allowing his observer, Second Lieutenant R. V. Walker, to open fire with his front Lewis gun. The Fokker pilot began to climb, but Doune climbed with him and Walker fired again, and so did Doune, with a fixed Lewis gun he had mounted on the right side of his cockpit. The Fokker had one of its wings rip away and it fell into the British lines. Much was later written about the 'Knights of the Air', but in this instance it was strangely true for Lord Doune had brought down Unteroffizier Georg Wilhelm Freiherr von Saalfeld. The Fokker came from FA18, the pilot being the son of Prince Ernst von Sachsen-Meiningen. Earlier that month Lord Doune and another pilot, each flying a Bristol Scout, had been getting the upper hand in a scrap with another Fokker but, at the crucial moment, both men's guns jammed.

April 1916 saw 24 Squadron begin making claims against the German Air Service. Second Lieutenants D. M. Tidmarsh and S. J. Sibley destroyed an Albatros C on the 2nd, then David Tidmarsh claimed a Fokker on the 30th, but he did not shoot it down. He was escorting FE2s, coming from Bapaume, over Péronne. He dived to attack but was never able to get close enough to open fire. However, the Fokker pilot, possibly in a panic, dived and appeared to lose control at about 1,000 feet. Unable to recover, he crashed into some houses in Combles. It was probably Leutnant Otto Schmedes of FA18 who was killed.

On 4 May the squadron claimed a two-seater, shot down by Second Lieutenant S. E. Cowan. Then, on the 16th, Lieutenant A. M. Wilkinson claimed two enemy machines shot down out of control, one an AGO GII, the other a Fokker. Lieutenant C. M. B. Chapman destroyed an LVG. All the above named became aces with 24 Squadron and helped wrest control of the air from the Fokkers during the early summer of 1916.

The Martinsyde G100s were only supplied to 27 Squadron in France and their first loss came on 20 May. Second Lieutenant M. D. Basden attacked a German two-seater, but its gunner's fire was more effective and Basden fell to his death. However, the new DH2 fighters would quickly make their mark and help defeat the Fokker menace.

A French Voisin equipped with a 38mm cannon in the front cockpit. It was brought down by Wilhelm Frankl of Kek Vaux on 10 January 1916 for his second victory. Its crew, from 36 CA (Section d'Avions Canon du 36° Corps d'Armée) were captured.

A BE2c and a Morane Parasol. This BE (4107) of 15 Squadron, was shot down by Oberleutnant Michael Krug of Kek 1, on 19 January 1916, its pilot being wounded. His observer, Second Lieutenant W. A. Brooking, the son of Brigadier General H. T. Brooking CB, was killed. Unfortunately, the gunners/observers in these BE2 machines sat in the front cockpit and so were less able to operate their Lewis gun, while the pilot's back was even more vulnerable to gunfire from behind.

Vfw Wass of FA3 stands in the observer's cockpit of this FE2b of 20 Squadron that he shot down on 29 February 1916. His Fokker is on the left because it was not unknown for a victorious pilot to land by his victim, provided they were well back from the lines so as not to attract Allied artillery fire.

Immelmann's ninth victory, on 2 March 1916, a Morane BB of 3 Squadron. Both crewmen died, but not before the pilot had effected this landing.

Erbeutetes französisches Flugzeug

The captured crew of a 20 Squadron FE2b are driven away after being brought down on 9 March 1916. A Fokker had hit their engine forcing them down but unfortunately the identity of the German pilot is unknown.

Immelmann's thirteenth victory, another BE, and another loss for 15 Squadron, on 30 March 1916. The pilot was killed in the air but the observer, Lieutenant W. Joyce, although wounded, managed to crash-land the machine to begin his time as a prisoner.

The wrecked BE (2097) from 9 Squadron, shot down by Rudolf Berthold of Kek Vaux, on 16 April 1916. It was his fifth victory. The pilot was killed, the observer wounded and made a prisoner.

The burnt-out remains of Immelmann's fourteenth victory, an FB5 of 11 Squadron, 23 April 1916. Both crew men were taken prisoner.

The pilots of FA62 in 1916. Front row l. to r.: Salffener, Meding, Albert Österreicher, Oswald Boelcke, Hptm Hermann Kastner, Max Immelmann, von Krause, Ernst Hess. Rear: Max Mulzer, von Schilling, Max von Cossel, Fromme, von Gusner.

Oswald Boelcke flying over the front in a Fokker EIV. Note some trench works, top right-hand corner.

Lord Doune MC, who, with his observer, brought down a Fokker Eindecker which fell into British lines on 29 April 1916. They were flying an FE2b of 25 Squadron.

David Tidmarsh, of 24 Squadron, came from Limerick and was born in 1892. Earlier he had served with the Royal Irish Regiment. He and Lieutenant S. J. Sibley made the first claim for the squadron on 2 April 1916.

Jack Cunningham, who claimed his first three victories in an FB5, a Bristol Scout and a DH2. Later in the war he would fly Sopwith Camels and command 65 Squadron, ending the war as a lieutenant colonel, commanding No. 65 Wing, with the DSO, DFC and CdG and a ten-victory ace.

Jean Navarre in front of his Nieuport Scout with Escadrille N67.

Navarre flying in his distinctively marked red, white and blue Nieuport 11 Scout over Verdun, April 1916. Note the top-wing-mounted machine gun.

Navarre in another of his Nieuport Scouts, clearly showing a machine gun fitted in front of the cockpit, obviously with an interrupter gear installed.

A Martinsyde G100 'Elephant' which equipped 27 Squadron. Although designated as a fighter and bomber, it was not successful in the former role, but the squadron did fly many bomb raids.

Kurt Student, commander of a Fokkerstaffel with III Armée in 1916. He would achieve three victories flying a Fokker and later commanded one of the new Jastas. In the Second World War he commanded Germany's airborne forces. Note the rear-view mirror on the port support strut, two machine guns and the head-rest behind the cockpit.

Chapter Four
Fokker Aces Supreme

By mid-1916 the Fokker menace dominated the Western Front; despite there being relatively few of them, the handful of successful pilots flying Fokkers ruled the sky. By the end of May Boelcke and Immelmann had eighteen and fifteen victories respectively. Kurt Wintgens downed his first victory of the year with a Nieuport Scout on 20 May and then a Caudron G4 on the 21st. He shot down two more French machines in June bringing his score to eight. On 1 July he was awarded the *Pour le Mérite*, the fourth fighter pilot so honoured. One week later, on the 8th, Max von Mulzer received the same decoration having scored steadily; one victory on 31 May, three in June (all FE2bs), then with two BE2c machines on 2 and 8 July, he reached the magic number of eight.

Gustav Leffers became an ace on 9 July, the same day that Otto Parschau gained his eighth victory. This latter was exceptional for a Fokker pilot, for it was a balloon. The Battle of the Somme had opened on 1 July and Parschau had been sent to this battle-front at the head of a Fokker section with FA32 to help the situation in the air. Obviously this observation balloon was helping to direct artillery fire against German troops and its destruction was observed by German front-line soldiers. The next day came the *Pour le Mérite*.

Otto Höhndorf got his eighth victory on 15 July, but his reward was a bit slower and by the time his *Pour le Mérite* was announced on the 20th, he had scored twice more, a Farman on the 19th and a Nieuport on the 21st. He made it eleven victories with a Martinsyde of 27 Squadron on the 31st.

Ernst von Althaus claimed his eighth on 21 July, a Farman, the same day his *Pour le Mérite* was announced. However, it was his final victory with Kek Vaux. His eyesight was becoming a problem, which would lead to his leaving the Air Service in 1917.

Hans Berr gained two victories with Kek Avillers in March 1916, after serving with the army and being wounded in September 1914. He started out as an observer but soon took pilot training. Kek Avillers later became a Jasta, and Berr commanded it, and shot down a further eight French and British aircraft, before a collision ended his life. He had, however, been awarded the *Pour le Mérite* on 4 December.

✳ ✳ ✳

By the spring of 1916, the arrival of 24 Squadron RFC, with its DH2 pusher fighters, began making the situation for the Fokker pilots more precarious. Pilots such as C. M. B. Chapman, A. G. Knight, J. O. Andrews, S. E. Cowan, H. C. Evans and A. M. Wilkinson were starting to put air supremacy once again in the hands of the RFC on the British front.

Alan Machin Wilkinson, from Eastbourne, Sussex, an Oxford graduate, had moved from the Hampshire Regiment to the RFC and joined 24 Squadron in January 1916. He began operating in France by carrying two Lewis guns, but was quickly ordered to use only one. After downing a two-seater and a Fokker on 16 May, he got another Fokker the next day. His sixth victory was another Fokker on 19 July. He would claim ten victories in all with 24 Squadron, and almost double this by the spring of 1917, flying Bristol Fighters with 48 Squadron; he was rewarded with the DSO and Bar.

British-born Arthur Gerald Knight lived much of his youth in Canada but returned when war began and, once a pilot, flew corps aircraft until moved to 24 Squadron. He downed two Fokkers in 1916 and by November had scored seven victories in all.

Sidney Edward Cowan, from Dublin, was an original member of 24 Squadron and his first five victories were all over two-seaters. His second, on 1 July, the first day of the Somme, was nearly his last. It had landed inside enemy territory and Cowan dived down to strafe it, but then his engine failed and he was forced to land also. Fortunately, he managed to get it restarted and got off before German troops arrived. He received the MC for this action.

Charles Meredith Bouverie Chapman, from Canterbury, had been a pre-war soldier, but transferred to the RFC in 1915. With 24 Squadron he claimed three victories, including two Fokkers, one from KG3 on 14 July, and the other on 20 July.

He would become an ace with 29 Squadron (Nieuports) in 1917 before his death following a bomb raid on his home airfield on 1 October.

Henry Cope Evans from Surrey had been born in 1879, so he was 35-years old when war began. He had served during the Boer War and lived in Canada until the First World War started. He then served in France with the 19th Alberta Dragoons. After pilot training he was with 24 Squadron and shot down five two-seaters, but was killed on 3 September 1916.

Meantime, the FE2b crews were taking their share of combat successes. Despite their lumbering appearance, these large two-seat pushers could give a good account of themselves in air fights with enemy aircraft. The pilot had a fixed forward-firing Lewis gun while his front-seat observer had two moveable Lewis guns, one for firing across an arc of 90 degrees from left to right, with the other on a telescopic mounting at the rear of the observer's cockpit, fitted to enable him to fire back over the top wing. To do this effectively, the man had to stand on his seat and reach up while his pilot might well be twisting and turning to avoid an attack from the rear. Several RFC squadrons used these machines, but the main fighting ones were Nos 11, 20, 22, 23 and 25. George Ranold Macfarlane Reid, from Ayrshire, was a former soldier who was wounded early in the war. Moving to the RFC he became a pilot with 25 Squadron where he and his observer, J.A. Mann (son of Sir John Mann), were both awarded MCs for their fighting prowess in 1916 (three victories) before Reid went to 20 Squadron. With other observers he added six more victories. Of his nine in total, three were over Fokkers. Mann was killed in action on 9 August. However, before this, Mann, flying with another future fighter ace, Noel William Ward Webb, shot down a Fokker on 19 July. Vizfeldwebel Otto Dappert of FA18 was their victim, his Fokker losing a wing as it plummeted to earth. Webb gained five victories with his various observers in 1916 and went on to be a successful Camel pilot (MC and Bar) in 1917 before falling to Werner Voss on 16 August.

* *

The Royal Naval Air Service (RNAS), by definition, was the air arm of the Royal Navy, its aeroplanes to be used for defending the fleet in home waters, patrolling the North Sea and Atlantic ocean for enemy ships and submarines, and operating along the Channel coast while based in northern France and Belgium. Most of its early aeroplanes would, of course, be seaplanes and floatplanes, although land 'planes, similar to the ones used by the RFC, were taken on strength. As the war progressed and the stalemate of the Western Front continued, more and more support was requested from the RFC, and, bit by bit, RNAS squadrons equipped with land planes operated from French bases along the British front.

Initially RNAS units were known as wings and a number of pilots operating with the RNAS would later become aces whilst supporting their RFC brothers. Among the first was Redford Henry Mulock, a Canadian from Winnipeg, born in 1886. He transferred to the RNAS from the Canadian field artillery in 1915 and quickly became a first-class leader, and one never to miss the opportunity to engage enemy aircraft. Flying Nieuports along the North Sea coast with 1 Wing, 'Red' was involved in a number of combats but, as some pilots had little reason to count so-called victories as a yardstick, he and others were only too pleased to see off hostile incursions; if they were seen to be damaged in some way, that was a bonus. His first recorded encounter that might be termed a success came on 30 December 1915, forcing a two-seater down 'out of control' over Dixmude. In January 1916 he forced a two-seater to land in its own territory, and claimed another 'out of control' near Nieuport. On 21 May he claimed two more C-types out of control, becoming, it could be said, the first Canadian ace. He received the DSO for air fighting, attacking ships and submarines, and for reconnaissance missions, as well as the French *Légion d'Honneur*. He later commanded a RNAS fighter squadron and was awarded a Bar to his DSO.

Australian Roderic Stanley Dallas was another early air fighter to gain fame with the RNAS. A pre-war soldier in the Australian Army he applied to be an aviator soon after war was declared. Rejected by the RFC, he was accepted by the RNAS in early-1915 and flew with 1 Wing at Dunkirk, flying recce sorties in both single- and two-seater aircraft. In the spring of 1916, now flying Nieuports, he claimed a C-type 'out of control' on 22 April, destroyed a seaplane off the Belgian coast on 20 May and then another C-type on the 21st. The RNAS, understanding that a better single-seat scouting machine was needed, agreed to test the new Sopwith Triplane fighter. One was attached to what was now referred to as A Squadron and, on 1 July 1916, he sent down another hostile machine. On the 9th, back in a Nieuport, he claimed a Fokker, thus gaining his fifth 'victory'. Number six came on 30 September, again in the Triplane. Dallas would later be credited with over thirty victories before his own death in action on 1 June 1918.

Daniel Murray Bayne Galbraith was another Canadian who learned to fly in America at his own expense before joining the RNAS. He began flying from Dover in May 1916 before moving to 1 Wing the following month. On 15 July, while flying a Nieuport, he attacked and set on fire a German seaplane off Ostend, and shot down another off Calais on 28 September. He then began flying a Sopwith Pup and by November had brought his score to six, flying with 8 Naval Squadron on the British front. He was awarded the DSC and Bar. Sadly he was killed in a car accident in 1921.

Stanley James Goble came from Victoria, Australia, and was born in 1891. He also flew with 1 Naval Wing with Nieuport and Pups. His first two victories were in the former and, like Murray Galbraith, he went to 8 Naval where he downed a further six German two-seaters, for which he received the DSC and, later, a DSO. He later commanded a RNAS bomber squadron in early-1918. In later life he became an air commodore with the Royal Australian Air Force (RAAF) and later an air vice marshal.

Christopher Draper flew Sopwith 1½ Strutters with 3 Wing in 1916. He had become a pilot in 1913 and joined the RNAS when war began. Flying these Sopwith two-seaters on escort duties, he and his various observers often encountered enemy aircraft and, in November 1916, he was credited with four victories, the first being one of the new Fokker D biplane fighters. He would later become an ace flying Sopwith Camels. Another pilot to begin a long run of combat victories with 3 Wing on Strutters was Canadian Raymond Collishaw. He claimed two scouts on 25 October 1916, but it was 1917 when he got into his stride with a further thirty-eight claims. This he added to in 1918, ending the war with sixty.

By late 1916, the RNAS had begun to organise aircraft into Naval squadrons. As already mentioned, one was No.8, and this unit saw one of the greats of aerial air fighting begin his run of successes late in the same year. Robert Alexander Little came from Melbourne, Australia, and was born in July 1895. He joined the RNAS in 1915 and began by flying Curtiss H-16 Large America seaplanes over the North Sea. In mid-1916 he was flying from Dunkirk in Bristol Scouts and going on bomb raids in Sopwith Strutters. Flying a Sopwith Pup on 23 November, he sent down a C-type in flames and in December gained two more 'victories'. When he was killed in May 1918 his score stood at forty-seven.

The Sopwith Pup was the latest single-seat scout to arrive on the Western Front and would see a good deal of action in 1917. However, in late 1916, it began arriving in Naval 8 for the RNAS pilots. It was a very pleasant aeroplane to fly but only carried one Vickers machine gun fitted in front of the pilot. No. 54 Squadron of the RFC began to receive Pups and took them to France in December.

Kurt Wintgens' fourth victory, a French Nieuport XII from N68, downed on 20 May 1916. Note that it does not carry French roundels on the upper wing, but clearly shows the flag insignia of N68 on the fuselage.

Ein am 20. 5. 16 in Wich abgestürztes franz. Flugzeug

Walter Höhndorf received the *Pour le Mérite* on 20 July 1916, having downed his eighth victory on the 15th. By the 20th he had downed another and would make it ten on the 22nd.

Fritz Bernert of Jasta 2, with pet, and Ernst von Althaus. Von Althaus received his 'Blue Max' on 21 July 1916, the day he got his eighth victory. Bernert, another ace to wear spectacles, would receive his on 24 April 1917. On that day he shot down five British aeroplanes in twenty minutes, bringing his score to twenty-four.

Von Althaus standing by his Fokker Eindecker. Note again the head-rest behind the cockpit. The machine gun has its protective canvas covering whilst on the ground and, judging by the amount of mud in the picture, it is clearly winter.

Oswald Boelcke standing in his Fokker EIV heavily clad in his leather jacket. Note his aircraft has twin machine guns.

One of Max Immelmann's Eindeckers, another EIV, with his two mechanics posing for the picture. Its number can be read as 127/16. Note that both these pictures show the EIV with holes in the cowling to aid cooling of the rotary engine.

Otto Parschau's Fokker EIII. The line of signal flares can be seen at the edge of the cockpit and the painted wheel covers are no doubt a form of personal markings so that he can be recognised in the air and from the ground.

Parschau and Hans von Keudell. The latter, after service with the army, had become a bomber pilot, and fought in Poland and during the Verdun battles. Moving to fighters, he was sent to Kek Bertincourt. He did not score any victories prior to the formation of the Jastas but, in the latter half of 1916, with Jasta 1, began to make a name for himself.

Oberleutnant Hans Berr. With Kek Avillers he scored two victories in March 1916 but, like von Keudell, began to shine with the coming of the Jastas, leading Jasta 5. His Blue Max came on 4 December 1916.

A flying shot of a DH2, of No. 41 Squadron, B Flight, with flight commander's pennants on each outer wing strut.

The Airco DH2 pusher scout. It carries a single fixed machine gun and spare ammunition drums are carried in panniers each side of the cockpit with two drums in each, a total of five in all. This machine was used by 32 Squadron's B Flight.

Lieutenant D. M. Tidmarsh of 24 Squadron in helmet, leather jacket and 'fug' boots. Note the ladder, bottom right, used to climb into the cockpit of the DH2 and also the nacelle damage sustained to the left of his head. This was caused by a shell that passed through the forward part of the cockpit area. The machine gun is fitted off-centre.

Lieutenant C. M. B. Chapman of 24 Squadron. His MC and other decorations have been painted on in this picture. He was killed by bomb splinters on 1 October 1917 and the day after his funeral (the 7th) his younger brother William, an observer with 22 Squadron, was killed in action, shot down by Jasta 36.

S. E. Cowan, 24 Squadron. He was awarded the MC and Bar for his actions prior to his death on 17 November 1916, following a collision. His brother, Captain P. C. Cowan, was killed on 7 November 1917 in an SE5 of 56 Squadron by the same pilot who shot down Chapman's brother, Hans von Haebler, Jasta 36.

A. G. Knight DSO MC became an ace flying DH2s with 24 and 29 Squadrons. He was killed in action on 20 December 1916, shot down by Manfred von Richthofen for his thirteenth victory.

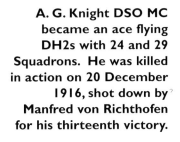

A. M. Wilkinson of 24 Squadron, showing the ribbon of the DSO with Bar. He gained ace status in 1916 and went on to claim nineteen victories on Bristol Fighters in 1917. He ended the war as a lieutenant colonel.

H. C. Evans DSO, 24 Squadron, in 1916. He was killed in action on 3 September having achieved five victories, at the age of thirty-six.

Two pilots from 24 Squadron in 1916. On the left is
R. H. M. S. Saundby who scored three victories in
1916. His fifth victory, for which he received the MC,
was over a Zeppelin airship in June 1917, flying on
Home Defence duties. In the Second World War he
was deputy commander of RAF Bomber Command.
On the right is Patrick A. Byrne from County Louth,
Ireland, although he preferred to be known as
Langan-Byrne. Flying DH2s with 24, he accounted
for ten victories in 1916, although seven of these
were of the 'forced to land' variety. However, it
brought him the DSO, but he was killed on 16
October, shot down by Oswald Boelcke, the
German's thirty-fourth victory.

J. O. Andrews of 24 Squadron claimed
twelve victories in the First World War, the
first seven flying DH2s. Awarded the MC
and Bar, he retired from the RAF as an air
vice marshal. Although he wears Scottish
headgear, having served with the Royal
Scots, he came from Lancashire and was
born in 1896.

A group of RNAS I Wing pilots in 1916. In the centre front is Red Mulock while seated in the front, on the right, is Stanley Dallas. In front on the left is Lieutenant D. C. S. Evill, from New South Wales, Australia, later Air Chief Marshal Sir Douglas Evill GBE KCB DSC AFC.

D. M. B. Galbraith DSO, I Wing RNAS, from Ontario.

J. Goble **DSO DSC**, from Victoria, Australia, flew Nieuport Scouts with 1 Wing and, later, 8 Naval Squadron, flying Sopwith Pups.

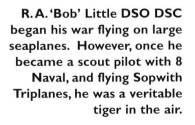

R. A. 'Bob' Little **DSO DSC** began his war flying on large seaplanes. However, once he became a scout pilot with 8 Naval, and flying Sopwith Triplanes, he was a veritable tiger in the air.

Stanley Dallas standing on the wheel of a Bréguet 2 at Coudekerque in the spring of 1916. His companion is Flight Sub Lieutenant G. V. Leather. Note the bomb racks under the starboard wing, the petrol tank on the cross wires, an early kind of wheel chock between Leather's feet and the petrol cans. The machine appears to be well tied down too.

Dallas in front of a Nieuport II 'Bebe' while with I Naval Wing in 1916.

Future ace Flight Sub-Lieutenant Chris Draper seated in a French Deperdussin monoplane. Note the car-like steering wheel and the inverted V-struts to accommodate the wires for wing-warping.

Another pilot to begin his flying career with 1 Wing was E. W. Norton. In a Nieuport II he shot down a kite balloon on 20 October 1916. From North Wales, Norton later served with 6 Naval and became an ace in 1917. This is a 1917 picture, but the wing gun position is clear.

BE2c 4196 brought down by Wilhelm Frankl on 1 July 1916. This victory is sometimes missed off his victory list and, depending on how one interprets it, it was approximately his seventh victory. The pilot of this 12 Squadron machine was Second Lieutenant L. A. Wingfield who was captured, but escaped in October 1917. For this effort, Wingfield received the MC in 1919, although prior to this, he had been awarded the DFC in 1918.

Chapter Five
Knights of the Air

By mid-1916 the French and German civilian population were well aware of their air heroes battling on the Western Front. They were the modern knights, jousting among the clouds with chivalry as their watchword. There were undoubtedly moments of being chivalrous to an opponent but, in the main, a dead opponent was better than a live one who, on the morrow, could come back and do you or a comrade serious harm. By this time it was clear to both sides that the best way of attacking an enemy in the air was to make an approach without the other seeing you. The best scenario was that the enemy had no idea you were close enough to fire until bullets were actually ripping into craft or body. There was nothing chivalrous in this. It was akin to shooting someone in the back. Yet the fighter pilots who were doing this sort of thing successfully were the modern heroes of the First World War.

Both the French and Germans publicised their air heroes. There was that certain something that put them above mere soldiers on the ground, struggling in the mud and carnage of the trenches. Names such as Guynemer, Nungesser and Navarre, were as famous as today's pop singers, their photographs in all the newspapers, and aviation and war magazines. In Germany too, their fighting airmen became household names: Boelcke, Immelmann, Wintgens and Parschau were equally well known. The Sanke Postcard Company even produced posed portraits of these heroes that were collected and purchased enthusiastically. Britain, on the other hand, rarely lionised her air heroes. This would, it was felt, be detrimental to all the other servicemen, each doing his best to win this terrible war.

Therefore it was up to the journalists to investigate who in the RFC and RNAS were creating mayhem against the 'Hun'. Every now and again a newspaper would try to bring the name of the latest event that involved some heroic action by a fighting pilot, and someone somewhere began to note a victory score to a famous name. It was like noting a footballer's goal score as a yardstick of his prowess, ignoring the rest of the team who were helping to make it possible for the 'hero' to score. Most of the fighter pilots were officers, and the war had produced a new gallantry award for acts of heroism for officers and warrant officers, the Military Cross (NCOs and soldiers received the Military Medal). Awards of this decoration would be promulgated in the pages of the *London Gazette*, often with a citation, and this citation might say that this pilot had managed to shoot down a number of aircraft. It was in this way that pilot scores began to be recorded, and so-called aces emerged. The French had first used a reference to a pilot becoming an ace if he had shot down five enemy aircraft. Armchair historians continued to use this title in reference to other pilots. Sometimes, of course, an outstanding performance would transcend the 'stiff upper lip' of Britain's high command, and a name became public knowledge. One such name was Albert Ball.

Albert Ball came from Nottingham and, in early 1916, he was only 19 years old. Having transferred to the RFC from the Sherwood Foresters, he had begun to fly two-seaters in February 1916, then moved to 11 Squadron which had some Nieuport Scouts. He joined this squadron on 7 May. Ball was killed exactly one year later, but in that year he received the MC, followed by the DSO and two Bars. No doubt he was proud of this, but he was not a medal chaser as some later became. His first combat victory came on 16 May, driving down a two-seater in a Bristol Scout, but his next two on 29 May were in a Nieuport.

Later historians would record that Ball destroyed forty-three German aircraft and one balloon, but once again this has to be viewed by the terminology of the day. Ball often flew lone sorties, hunting out the enemy, intent on attacking anything German he found in the sky, but he knew his main job was to deprive the enemy of its reconnaissance potential. If he drove away or 'drove down' enemy two-seaters, he was helping to save British lives on the ground. Driving down a reconnaissance machine does not sound particularly useful, but it had taken that two-seater some time to gain the height at which Ball attacked and, if driven well down, it might well take too long for its crew to climb up again, so they would be forced to abandon their task. Even hitting the enemy machine with a few bullets might have damaged the aircraft sufficiently for the crew to abandon the job in hand, and may have even wounded or killed one of them. Even when the enemy machine was seen to 'force land' behind its own lines counted as a victory, for again, either crew member could be dead or dying, or the aircraft seriously damaged.

Ball, of course, did record some victories as destroyed, and many of his opponents he listed as LFG Roland CII types, a distinctive looking machine. Ball was a shy, almost reclusive figure. While he would share the camaraderie with his squadron pals, he would prefer his own company, and often did. In August 1916 he moved to 60 Squadron, again flying Nieuport Scouts, and continued to fly off alone. Trying to confirm his victories was unimportant to him, although he did note a personal tally from time to time, but others in the air would see some German aircraft go tumbling down knowing Ball was probably in that part of the sky, and reports from the front line would confirm what he claimed. His own combat reports rarely embellished what had occurred, but he was credited with victory after victory, so that by mid-September 1916, when he was rested, this score stood at thirty-one, although broken down into types of victory, this should read: sixteen destroyed, five out of control, nine forced to land, plus one balloon.

He remained something of an enigma while with 60 Squadron, even having his own hut in front of which he had a small garden which he enjoyed tending. He was liked and admired by his comrades. In the air he was awesome. He had studied what was the best way of attacking enemy aircraft, and was a born hunter. Knowing the two-seat gunner in the aircraft he was going for generally took less care in looking immediately below his machine, Ball would try to keep in the man's blind spot and gradually climb up beneath his opponent. Pulling down the top-wing Lewis gun, he got into position and opened fire.

* *

Mentioning Ball's victory over a balloon, it should be remembered that these dangerous targets were often ignored by some pilots, especially those who had gained experience in air fighting. Others, of course, seemed to be obsessed with attacking them, and, oddly enough, became adept at doing so. Although they were sometimes attacked with ordinary bullets, on planned attacks a gun would be loaded with incendiary ammunition so as to ignite the balloon's contents. In 1916 another method of destroying balloons was employed, rockets designed by a French naval officer, Yves Le Prieur. On the Nieuport, four rockets were placed in tubes on each of the wing's V-struts. The idea was to head for the balloon, fire off the rockets and hope they would hit. They had a few successes but, in 60 Squadron, Lieutenant E. J. L. W. Gilchrist destroyed one on 15 September 1916 while a companion, against orders, fired his off against an LVG two-seater which he hit and set on fire. On the 26th Lieutenants G. Phillippi and R. M. Hill each bagged a balloon using rockets. Euan Gilchrist would command a squadron later in the war, and Roderic Hill later rose to air chief marshal. Hill, George Phillippi and Gilchrist each were awarded the MC for these actions. Like so many similar events, decorations came for first-time successes.

The German Fokker pilots were still making their presence felt but their days were coming to an end. The DH2 and Nieuport Scouts were starting to dominate, and then disaster. On 18 June 1916 the great Max Immelmann fell. That evening he was out with some companions following a report that eight FE2b machines had crossed the lines. They found 25 Squadron and Immelmann attacked first, hitting one plane and wounding its pilot and observer, forcing them to make a rapid landing. Returning to base the Fokkers had hardly refuelled when another British formation was reported. Immelmann had had his Fokker slightly damaged in the first fight so was up in another, an EIII (246/16), so not his usual EIV. Attacking this second 25 Squadron formation, Immelmann's fire hit the FE, again wounding both crewmen, one fatally, and it crashed near Lens.

Seeing the FE in trouble, another crew, Second Lieutenant G. R. McCubbin and Corporal J. H. Waller, tried to assist, Waller opening fire on the Fokker. No sooner had he done so than both men saw the Fokker stagger, begin to go down and then start to fall to pieces. Immelmann crashed near Sallaumines, falling from 2,000 metres. From that day controversy has raged over what had happened. The British crew were credited with one Fokker destroyed and, later, when it became known who its pilot had been, McCubbin was awarded the DSO and Waller the DCM. The Germans reported that Immelmann, while attacking the FE, had a malfunction with his interrupter gear, and shot off one propeller blade, resulting in a severe vibration that shook the Fokker apart. From this distance it is impossible to divide the two accounts, and while one must accept the findings of the German who inspected the wreckage, German propaganda would prefer this version rather than their hero having been bested in combat. The question, of course, is why, as soon as Immelmann realised he had a problem, did he not shut down the engine and proceed to glide down? Had he been wounded by Waller's fire, and/or had Waller also hit the propeller?

Immelmann was never officially credited with his final two victories, although Max Mulzer appears to have claimed the second FE for his fourth victory. Perhaps it was a case of 'if nobody can have it, I will'. Mulzer went on to claim ten victories by early August. Before that, however, Otto Parschau received mortal wounds in combat on 21 July after eight victories, and Gustav Leffers did not survive the year, although he had moved away from the Fokker, and was sometimes flying a captured Nieuport Scout.

Within days, Boelcke, having scored his nineteenth victory on 27 June, was taken away from the front, High Command not wanting to risk another death among its hero elite. Although the Fokkers continued to fly over the front for several more weeks, the high-water mark of their success had ended, but new aircraft and a better organisation was just around the corner. If the Allied air forces thought they were gaining the upper hand, they would soon be disillusioned.

* *

On the French front the Battle of Verdun was still in progress just as the Somme battles still raged further to the north. Squadrons were starting to emerge in both Allied air forces, equipped with just one type of fighter. They were also being formed within set formations such as wings or groups attached to various armies. By the end of the year the French would be using *Groupes de Combat* (GC) with several escadrilles lumped together.

By the summer of 1916, names such as Guynemer and Nungesser were well known. At the end of September, Guynemer had been credited with eighteen victories, Nungesser with seventeen. Other names were coming to the fore. Rene Pierre Marie Dorme came from two-seaters to join N3, gaining his first victory on 9 July. By September this had become twelve, all two-seaters. Andre Chainat was still flying with N3, but was wounded on 7 September, although he had achieved eleven victories plus two probables. Alfred Heurtaux had eight victories with N3 by September, at which time a new fighter was being used by French fighter pilots, the Spad VII. A short time later N3 changed its designation to Spa3. On 25 September Heurtaux shot down a Fokker EIV piloted by Kurt Wintgens. The Frenchman's fire hit the Fokker's fuel tank, causing the machine to explode. So ended the life of Wintgens after gaining nineteen victories. The following day von Mulzer was killed in a flying accident. His success had brought him the title of Ritter

(Knight) and *von*. He had been the first Bavarian ace and the first fighter pilot to be knighted.

Marcel Robert Leopold Bloch, born in Switzerland, was 26 years old. Flying with N62 he scored five victories between 26 June and 1 October 1916 – all of them balloons. Jean Chaput, from Paris, flew with N57 having already seen action with a two-seater unit, claiming a Fokker on 12 June 1915, and after being wounded, served with Groupement d'Angers in March 1916, where he shot down another Fokker on 30 April. Moving to N57 he had a total of eight victories by the end of July and would score sixteen before his death in combat in 1918. A brother pilot in N57 was Victor Louis Georges Sayaret. A former dragoon, his first victory, a German machine which he forced to land, came while flying a Voisin with V24. He then went on to single-seaters with N57 and scored five more victories in 1916. Noel Hugues Anne Louis de Rochfort scored seven victories with N26 in 1916, but was shot down by anti-aircraft fire, wounded and captured on 15 September; he died the next day.

Albert Louis Deullin, born in Epernay in August 1890, had entered military service in 1912, serving with the dragoons until 1915 when he became a pilot. His first assignment was with MF62 where he claimed one victory on 10 February 1916. Going to N3, his third official victory was over a Fokker that came down in French lines on 31 March. Deullin would eventually claim ten victories by the end of 1916, and double this by 1918.

Another early ace, who had scored two victories in 1915 whilst flying two-seaters with C18, was Maxime Albert Lenoir, born in December 1888. He flew Nieuports with N23 in 1916, his first claim being a Fokker on 17 March, adding another of these on 30 July. On 25 September he gained his eleventh victory, despite being wounded on 9 August, and on this September day. Returning to duty he was killed in action on 23 October flying a Spad VII.

Paul Joannes Sauvage, born in February 1897, became a pilot in March 1916. Sent to N65 as a caporal, he quickly achieved rank and victories, downing his fifth on 2 October, thus becoming the youngest French ace at the age of 19. His score had risen to eight with four more probables by the end of the year, by which time he was flying with N38. Back with N65, his fighter received a direct hit from an anti-aircraft shell on 7 January 1917, and he was killed.

Another name that became well known was Paul Albert Pierre Tarascon, born in 1882. He joined the military in 1901. Learning to fly in 1911 he had a serious accident but this obviously did not deflect him, even though he had to have his right foot amputated. When war came he immediately applied for pilot training and received his brevet by the end of 1914. However, no doubt due to his disability, he was tasked with being an instructor, but this did not suit him and after some badgering he managed to be assigned to N31, then N2 and, finally, N62 where he scored his first victory on 15 July. He became an ace on 15 September and raised his total to eight by the year end. By 1918 he had scored a total of twelve victories, with some twelve more as probables. He was known as *'l'as la jambe de bois'* – the ace with the wooden leg. In the Second World War, Tarascon was in action with the French Resistance.

Marcel Pierre Vialet, from Lyon, born in August 1887, had already travelled the world when war came and was wounded fighting as a *cuirassier*. This projected him into flying and by March 1916 he was flying Caudrons. He and his gunner claimed a Fokker on 28 April. Re-assigned to fighters, he went to N67 and scored nine victories by December, with another eight probables. Georges Charles Marie Francois Flachaire also flew with N67 at the same time and accounted for eight German aircraft in 1916.

There was one other unit now flying for France, this being the Lafayette Escadrille or, officially, N124. It was commanded by French officers, but was made up of American volunteers. Although rather glamorised by post-war writers, it was nevertheless an aggressive outfit with a number of interesting characters among its personnel. Not the least of these was Gervais Roual Victor Lufbery, also known as Roual. He was in fact born in France, of an American father and French mother. He ran away from home when aged 17 and over the next four years spent time in several middle eastern countries. In 1906, when he was 21, he went to America, joined the army and spent two years of active service in the Philippines. He then travelled to the Far East, seeing his first aeroplane in Cochin China in 1910. Later he became a mechanic to the French aviator Marc Pourpe in 1912. Pourpe returned to France with Lufbery when war began, but to serve in the military he had to join the French Foreign Legion, as did other American volunteers. When Pourpe was killed, Lufbery joined the air service and became a pilot in July 1915. Initially flying Voisins, when the Lafayette was formed he joined it. He shot down his first German on 30 July 1916 and by the end of the year his score stood at six.

Wilhelm Frankl received the *Pour le Mérite* on 12 August 1916, serving with Kek Vaux, after nine victories. By April 1917, by which time he was flying with Jasta 9, his score had risen to twenty.

Hartmut Baldamus flew Fokkers with FA20, achieving five victories by the end of July 1916. He would die in a collision with a French fighter in April 1917 after scoring eighteen victories. He would have been nominated for the Blue Max in December, but the rules had changed so that a pilot needed sixteen victories before this could be considered. His death prevented his nomination being processed.

Hans Berr flying his Eindecker near
Verdun in 1916 while with Kek Avillers.

Gustav Leffers wearing
his Blue Max, Iron Cross
First and Second Class,
Knight's Cross of the
Hohenzollern House
Order and two classes of
the Oldenburg-Freidrich-
August Cross.

Rudolf Berthold wearing the Iron Cross First Class on his tunic and the Second Class with the ribbon through a button hole. This latter medal was only displayed on the day of presentation and from then on just the ribbon would be shown. Berthold would receive the Blue Max on 12 October 1916 after his eighth victory. As a Bavarian he is wearing the Bavarian Flying Badge.

Albert Ball DSO MC. He achieved many combat successes, often flying alone over enemy territory. A supreme hunter and as brave as a lion, he survived months of front-line combat. In 1917, as a flight commander with 56 Squadron, he met his death and was awarded a posthumous Victoria Cross one month later.

One of Ball's Nieuport Scouts – A134; he flew these with 11 Squadron in May 1916.

Max Immelmann. At his throat is the Commander's Cross of the Military St Henry Order, Saxony's highest award for distinguished service and bravery. The *Pour le Mérite* is below and to the left. Other decorations are the Knight's Cross of the Military St Henry Order, the Knight Second Class with Swords of the Albert Order, the Friedrich August Medal in Silver, the Iron Cross Second Class, the Knight's Cross with Swords of the Royal Hohenzollern House Order, the Bavarian Military Merit Order, Fourth Class with Swords, and the Hanseatic Cross.

The 25 Squadron FE2b brought down by
Immelmann on 18 June 1916, the day he
fell in combat to another FE of this
squadron. The picture shows the wings of
this machine being dismantled.

Lieutenant G. R. McCubbin was
awarded the DSO for his part in
shooting down Max Immelmann
on 18 June 1916. The German
ace died in the crash.

Hans Berr, standing third from the right, with men of his Kek Avillers in June 1916. Others identified are in the seated row (l to r): Vfw Heinrich Büssing, Vfmst Max Winkelmann, Vfw Hans Müller (a future ace), Offz Paul Piechl (KIA 10 October 1916), unknown.

A French Nieuport Scout with a propeller boss fitted, which the French called a *cone de penetration*. This streamlined the machine in an effort to produce a higher speed. Albert Ball also used a similar device, painted bright red, on one of his Nieuports. In 1917 James McCudden, the British ace, also used this type of streamlining on his SE5A which he, too, painted red. Mick Mannock had a yellow one on his Nieuport 17.

Georges Guynemer wearing the medals of his Légion d'Honneur, Médaille Militaire and Croix de Guerre. The latter has four '*palmes*' appended, one for each time he was cited for a particular action. The ribbon of this medal became longer and longer the more citations a man received. At one stage, Guynemer had twenty-six *palmes* affixed to his. Rather like the German aces, Frenchmen such as Guynemer might receive any number of foreign decorations the more famous they became. At one time he was able to wear some ten, including the British DSO and the Ordre de Léopold.

Another well decorated French aviator, Charles Nungesser. Among his medals is the British Military Cross. Nungesser was rarely free from some injury or other and it is said that at one time or other he had broken virtually every bone in his body, at least once. He is standing by a Nieuport.

Nungesser in his Nieuport. His macabre personal marking on the fuselage shows a black heart, edged in white, with a skull and crossbones, a coffin and two brass candlesticks. He even had this insignia monogrammed on his shirts. As he continued to return to combat after each injury, he became known as 'The Indestructible'.

Maxime Lenoir with his N23 Nieuport which carries his name in red, white and blue, and a white band round the fuselage. He had scored eleven victories before falling in combat on 25 October 1916.

Rene Dorme flew with N3. Again we see the Legion d'Honneur, Medaille Militaire and Croix de Guerre on his breast. Above it is the white enamel stork insignia, denoting a member of the famous Storks Group (GC12). By the end of 1916 he had achieved seventeen victories and five probables. He would eventually claim twenty-three, plus seventeen probables, during 120 combats.

Dorme's Nieuport, numbered '12', during a visit and inspection by the French General Joseph Joffre, the French Chief of Staff.

Two of Dorme's comrades in N3 were Albert Deullin and Paul Tarascon, seen here with a red stork-marked Nieuport, which has a machine gun forward of the pilot's cockpit. Deullin scored ten of his eventual twenty victories in 1916, while Tarascon accounted for eight of his eventual twelve in this year.

Alfred Heurtaux, with his Legion d'Honneur medal and the stork einsignia. His variation of the *palmes* on his Croix de Guerre shows he had been cited twelve times, and received two *étoiles* (stars) in bronze. He scored 16 victories in 1916 of an eventual twenty-one.

Matheiu Tenant de la Tour flew with N57 and N3, with eight of his nine victories shot down in 1916, including two balloons. He was killed in a flying accident in December 1917.

One of Guynemer's Nieuport 11s in March 1916 during the Battle of Verdun. Guynemer himself is inspecting its engine. French roundel markings are on the undersides of both wings.

In contrast this Nieuport does not carry any upper-wing roundels. Capitaine Compte J. L. V. De Plane Sleyes De Seynes of N26 was brought down in this machine and captured on 3 July 1916 during a successful attack on a balloon. The insignia of N26, a flaming torch, is clear to see. Note, too, the light edging to wings and elevators.

Three French aces, Heurtaux, Guynemer and Tenant de la Tour, standing with Yves Le Prieur, the inventor of the anti-balloon rockets. Behind them is a Nieuport Scout of Escadrille N3, with its stork emblem painted in red.

A 60 Squadron Nieuport Scout with Le Prieur rockets, four on each wing-strut. They were used for attacking kite balloons, but could be very much a hit-or-miss affair.

Chapter Six
Nieuport Scouts

With the arrival at the front in the summer of 1915 of the Nieuport Scout, a machine that in various designations was to serve long and hard with both the French and the British in France, the first few were distributed among front-line escadrilles, and MS3 was one of them. When the unit was almost fully equipped with them, MS3 became N3. Guynemer began flying the Nieuport, designed by Gustave Delage of the late Édouard de Niéport's aeroplane company. It had a normal-sized upper wing, but the lower ones were much smaller in breadth, known as the sesquiplane design. The problem of the propeller was solved by placing a machine gun on the top wing, set to fire over the blades.

Patrolling was still in its comparative infancy and the number of serviceable aircraft in each unit made it impossible to mount large groups even if it was deemed necessary. Many pilots, once they had gained a modicum of experience, felt far happier to fly lone sorties and, of course, the opposition numbers were likewise still curtailed, so a lone aviator was unlikely to run into a mob of hostile adversaries.

Before Guynemer got into his stride he was lucky to survive a crash on 30 November 1915, his Nieuport 10 turning over when attempting to get down. However, before the year was out, he had secured three victories on the Nieuport, two being two-seater observation aeroplanes, the third being a Fokker, on 14 December. Already the holder of the Médaille Militaire, Guynemer was made a Chevalier de la Légion d'Honneur on 24 December.

Charles Eugene Jules Marie Nungesser was, like Guynemer, Paris born, on 15 March 1892 and so was about two years older than Guynemer. He enlisted into a Hussar regiment when war began and, before transferring to aviation, had won the Médaille Militaire. Trained to be a pilot in March 1915, he was sent to Escadrille VB106 (Voisin). He was involved in a fight with an Albatros in the early morning of 31 July over Nancy, thus achieving his first victory in combat. No doubt this aggression led to him being sent to a scouting Escadrille, N65, another recently equipped with Nieuport Scouts. He claimed his first single-seat victory on 4 December, having been made a Chevalier de la Légion d'Honneur the previous day. Even at this stage of the war, decorations were awarded for feats that within months would be deemed commonplace.

Any number of two-seater pilots and observers would later transfer to fighter aeroplanes. Not least among them were Bruno Loerzer and his observer, Hermann Wilhelm Göring. Loerzer was a former army cadet, born in January 1891 at Friedenau, near Berlin. He had begun to take flying lessons shortly before the war started and by October 1914 was sent to FA25. Soon to join him was brother army officer Hermann Göring, who flew as his observer. Göring came from Rosenheim, Upper Bavaria, the son of a distinguished army officer who, in addition, had been the Governor of German South-West Africa. When the war began he served on the Vosges front but suffered from rheumatoid arthritis and, after a period in hospital, decided he would be better off flying with his friend. Although they often flew together, Göring claimed victories with other pilots. The first was on 3 June 1915 but was not confirmed. His second claim, over a Farman near Tahure, brought him his first victory. Deciding to emulate his friend Leorzer he applied for pilot training and eventually returned to FA25 as a fully-fledged aviator. Göring, flying with Kek Metz, had three victories by the end of 1916.

* *

Nieuport Scouts had equipped No.1 Squadron RFC in August 1916 and as mentioned earlier, E. L. Foot MC was a flight commander. One prominent pilot was a Canadian, A. D. Bell-Irving, one of a family of boys serving in the First World War. His first victory was over a Roland C on 29 August while the Squadron still had several Moranes. During September and October he claimed three more Rolands, two more un-named two-seaters, and a balloon, receiving the MC. He was shot down on 9 November by Otto Höhne of Jasta 2, the German's fifth victory. Duncan Bell-Irving received a Bar to his MC but did not see further combat. There were four Bell-Irving pilots in the RFC and RNAS, and two more lads in the Army.

The tiny contingent of Belgian fighter pilots operating on the Channel coast had also started to produce aces. They had a very strict confirmation process, so that, while a number of pilots claimed several German aircraft shot down, actual officially recognised victories were far fewer.

Prominent among them in the early days was Fernand Maximillian Leon Jacquet, born in 1888, into a wealthy landowning family. An army cadet in 1907, he was another who decided flying was for him and received his brevet in 1913. When war began he was flying Farman two-seaters and on 17 April 1915 he and his observer, Lieutenant H. Vindevoghel, shot down an Aviatik, it being the first enemy aircraft to be officially credited as destroyed by a Belgian. His next two claims were not upheld, but he scored successfully in 1916, flying with Lieutenant Louis Robin in the front cockpit.

Jan [Jean] Olieslagers claimed three victories in late 1915 but only one was made official, and that occurred on 12 September. He came from Antwerp and was born in 1883. In his early years he became a motorcyclist but, in 1909, he purchased a Blériot and between 1910 and 1913 entered several air contests, then took his machine to North Africa in 1914 to make demonstration flights. When war began he and his two brothers volunteered to serve with the Belgian Air Force. One brother was also a pilot, the other a mechanic, and between them they had three Blériot machines. Jan flew and fought till the end of the war, making 567 war flights and taking part in ninety-seven combats. He made twenty-three claims but only had six confirmed. Brother [Josef] Max Olieslagers carried out 179 war flights as a two-seater pilot.

Before leaving this chapter, Otto Kissenberth is worthy of a mention. A Bavarian from Landshut, born in 1893, he had joined the air service at the start of the war. As a two-seater airman with FA8 he was wounded in action during an air fight, later returning to FA9b (the 'b' denoting a Bavarian unit), operating with a background of the Austrian Tyrol. Flying on this southerly Alsace front, he was then serving with Kek Ensisheim.

On 12 October 1916, without specific orders, he had taken off after hearing a report that Allied bombers had been seen heading for the Mauser factory at Oberndorf, south-west of Stuttgart. Flying a Fokker DII he engaged British and French bombers, escorted by Sopwith two-seaters of the RNAS and Nieuport Scouts from the Lafayette Escadrille.

Kissenberth shot down three of the bombers, two of them French Farmans, before having to land to refuel. Off again, he met the formation on their way back and shot down a Bréguet V of No.3 Wing RNAS. Three victories in a day was an outstanding event at this stage. Kissenberth was to go on to gain nineteen victories by May 1918 and, although he had not reached the magic figure of twenty kills, received the Blue Max in June for his outstanding prowess in air combat. He was seriously injured in a crash flying a captured Sopwith Camel on 20 May.

This French pilot is demonstrating how a gun on the top wing of his Nieuport could be pulled down in order to fire upwards into the undersides of a German two-seater. It can also be reached in order to change an empty drum for a full one. Note, too, that this Nieuport also carried a Vickers machine gun set to fire through the propeller.

A. CHAINAT

9 Victoires

The French, too, had their fighting heroes depicted on postcards, sold widely in France during the war. Here Andre Chainat is described as an 'ace' and notes his score of nine victories, two short of his ultimate tally of eleven. The Légion d'Honneur, Médaille Militaire and Croix de Guerre medals adorn his chest, the latter showing eight *palmes* and two stars. The photographer has his name too, N. Manuel of Paris. A pilot with N3 of the Storks Groupe, Chainat also wears the 'Stork' emblem.

Marcel Hauss, flying Nieuports with N57 from late 1916, was born in Paris in 1890. He was involved in five successful combats, three shared with other pilots, winning the Médaille Militaire and Croix de Guerre, but was killed attacking a two-seater from FA46 over St Mihiel on 15 February 1917.

Gustave Douchy was born in 1893 and flew with N38 in 1916-17. By early 1918 he had achieved eight victories and five probable, including a balloon victory, before becoming a test pilot. His first two claims were in the summer of 1916.

A Nieuport 17 flown by Capitaine Alfred Auger of N3; picture taken at Villers Bretonneux, October 1916. Auger had two victories with N31 in 1916 before being badly injured in a crash. Returning to front-line duty he was assigned to N3.

Capitaine Alfred Auger achieved a total of seven victories and seven probables before being killed in action in 28 July 1917 as commanding officer of N3. He wears the number 31 on his hat in reference to his first escadrille, but has the stork emblem on his tunic.

Line-up of Nieuport Scouts of the Storks' Group in 1916.

Three 1916 French aces, Alfred Heurtaux (N3), Georges Flachaire (N67) and Marcel Viallet (N67). Flachaire and Viallet scored seven and nine victories respectively.

Two future aces and high-ranking German officers, Hermann Göring and Bruno Loerzer. They flew together as observer and pilot with FA25 in 1915, but both would become fighter aces later in the war. The aeroplane is an Albatros B two-seater.

Nieuport Scout flown by Raoul Lufbery of the Lafayette Ecadrille (N124) in 1916 with a reference to his name on the fuselage.

Another view of Lufbery's Nieuport. The centre section of the upper wing has been altered to provide a clear view above and forward of the pilot's cockpit.

William (Bill) Thaw's Nieuport with the Lafayette Escadrille marked with the letter 'T'. Note the rear-view mirror to the right of the cockpit edge, with another directly above the cockpit. His flying helmet is clipped to the port wing wires.

Raoul Lufbery. Apart from his three French decorations, he also wears the British Military Medal far right. He was the highest scoring ace with the Lafayette Escadrille.

Bill Thaw by his Nieuport. Thaw scored just one victory in 1916 with the Lafayette, a Fokker EIII on 24 May, but became an ace in 1918. When America came into the war he rose to command the US 3rd Pursuit Group in France with the rank of lieutenant colonel.

Nungesser's Nieuport Scout while he was briefly attached to the Lafayette Escadrille in July 1916. The machine is camouflaged, but the light-coloured wing-edging is still visible. As well as a wing-mounted Lewis gun, the plane carries a machine gun firing through the propeller.

Jan Olieslagers of the Belgian 2nd Escadrille seated in a Nieuport two-seater that has been converted to a single-seater scout. This picture shows clearly the rotary engine whirling round. It is not always appreciated that the engine spun round with the propeller.

Olieslagers flying a Nieuport XI 'Bébé'. The machine is camouflaged, not normally the case with Belgian scouts.

Capitaine Fernand Jacquet of the Belgian Air Force scored all his victories flying two-seaters and was the first Belgian pilot to have a confirmed victory over a German aeroplane, an Aviatik two-seater on 17 April 1915. He also became the first Belgian ace and, on one occasion, flew King Albert of The Netherlands to the front lines.

Jan Olieslagers scored his first three victories in a Nieuport 10, but as two were only seen to fall apparently 'out of control' they were not allowed. Pre-war he met Roland Garros, a man with a similar outlook on flying. His Nieuport carries two Lewis guns on the top wing. While this doubled the fire power it also hindered speed and manoeuvrability in combat. Both guns are firmly attached so he would not be able to change the ammunition drums.

Three of 60 Squadron's Nieuport pilots, A. S. M. Summers, A. D. Bell-Irving MC and F. E. Goodrich MC. Alfred Summers shot down a balloon using Le Prieur rockets in September 1916, but this 30-year-old was killed in action on the 15th by Wilhelm Frankl for his eleventh victory. Bell-Irving achieved seven victories (Military Cross and Bar, Croix de Guerre). Frank Goodrich won his MC with 3 Squadron. An American from Maine, born in 1889, he died in a flying accident on 12 September 1916.

Otto Kissenberth learning his trade flying a Fokker EII with FA9b. Note the unorthodox flying hat. This Fokker, E33/15, was delivered to the unit on 21 August 1915.

Kissenberth after recovering from his injuries in May 1918, now wearing the Blue Max at his throat. He was yet another Great War aviator to wear spectacles.

Chapter Seven
Autumn Chill

Fokker Eindeckers were gradually withdrawn from the front, although they were still being met in the early autumn of 1916. With the approaching colder weather, there was another chill factor for the British and French air forces, the arrival of the Jastas.

It will be remembered that, following Immelmann's death, Oswald Boelcke had been withdrawn from active duty and sent on an inspection tour of aviation on other fronts. However, Boelcke was a thinking man as well as a superb air fighter, and had seen that the lack of sufficient numbers of fighters grouped together as units had caused problems. Rather than being scattered piecemeal with the two-seat *abteilungen*, he had put up a proposal that, with the coming of a number of new biplane fighters, these should be grouped together into fighting units, led by an experienced or, at least, a senior officer. Boelcke also knew that the airmen on the Western Front were meeting larger formations, especially of fighters, so there was an urgent need to rethink front-line policy.

The idea was to set up Jagstaffeln (each becoming known as a Jasta), comprised of around eight or nine pilots, led by a staffelführer. These were literally hunting units, tasked with engaging enemy aircraft over the front, or attacking those making incursions behind the German lines. This would, at the same time, hopefully give protection to German two-seater units operating across the front lines and would certainly engage would-be assailants of these reconnaissance aircraft. Boelcke himself was allowed to return to operational flying and given command of Jasta 2. To a degree he was allowed to hand pick his own men.

The new German aircraft that were now arriving from the factories were all biplanes, referred to as D-types (*doppeldecker*). Fokker had produced the DII and DIII, Albatros the DI and DII, and Halberstadt the DII, although the latter had become obsolete by the end of 1916. The Fokker biplanes had begun to replace

Eindeckers with the two-seater units just prior to the arrival of the Jastas and looked decidedly like a monoplane with another wing added. They, too, did not stay long, being outclassed by the Albatros and Halberstadt D-types. All these types were taken on the strength of the first fifteen Jastas that began forming, and apart from the Halberstadt, they carried twin Spandau machine guns. The Albatros and Halberstadt also had in-line engines rather than rotary.

Jasta 1 was formed on 22 August 1916, although Jasta 2's creation date was 10 August, as was Jasta 3. By the end of August there were seven, with eight more formed in September. All were designated Royal Prussian Jastas, but Jasta 16 was Royal Bavarian, that is to say it would be manned mainly by Bavarians. Further Jastas were also designated Royal Saxon and Royal Würrtemburg where, again, men from those states flew with them. Several were formed from former Kek or Kasta units.

When, in the last weeks of 1916, these Jastas began to get into their stride, flying mostly Albatros Scouts, with some Halberstadts, they quickly made their presence felt, although the winter weather started to curtail RFC operations to some extent. The spring of 1917 would be a very different story.

* *

On the British and French side the Nieuport seemed to alter its appearance and had become well established by this time. The DH2 continued operations and there was a similar-looking pusher fighter coming out from England, the FE8. A product of the Royal Aircraft Factory, it was slightly faster than the DH2, but when the first of them arrived in France it was felt that it was no real improvement over the DH2 and what was needed was a biplane such as the Germans were starting to acquire. One of two prototype FE8s, 7457, had been sent to France in January 1916, and attached to No.5 Squadron, which was flying Vickers FB5 two-seaters. It was taken over by Captain F. J. Powell MC. Fred Powell, from Manchester, served in the Manchester Regiment prior to joining the RFC. He was an aggressive pilot with 5 Squadron in 1915 and by the end of that year his record showed he had destroyed an AGO two-seater, 'driven' down three other C-types and 'driven off' three more. Not exactly victories but he had built a reputation and been decorated for his bravery. Now with a single-seater pusher, Powell became even keener on combat. On 17 January he claimed an Aviatik 'out of control'; on 5 February he drove down two two-seaters, drove off a third, and drove down another on the 7th. On the

29th he shot down an Aviatik in flames and on 12 March drove down a Fokker which trailed smoke from the engine as it went. This brought his tally to six 'victories' plus others driven down.

No. 40 Squadron was the first to arrive in France with FE8s, on 2 August, and 41 Squadron came along in October. Fred Powell, with his experience, became a flight commander with 40 Squadron. Captain D. O. Mulholland claimed 40's first two victories, both over Fokker Es, on 22 September and 20 October. On the 22nd the German pilot was Oberleutnant Karl Abert of Kek 3, the FE pilot shooting him down as he attacked an FE2b. The FE crew also claimed him, another reason why claims were sometimes duplicated. The FE crew, from 25 Squadron, were Sergeant T. Mottershead and Second Lieutenant C. Street. Tom Mottershead would win a posthumous Victoria Cross for an action on 7 January 1917.

Another victory claimed by 40 Squadron on 20 October, was a Roland 'out of control' by Lieutenant E. L. Benbow. Benbow got a two-seater in flames two days later, another on 14 November, a scout on 4 December, and finally a two-seater on 20 December. Edwin Benbow, from Abbotsbury, Dorset, had been an observer with 4 Squadron before he learned to fly. He was the only ace FE8 pilot, and scored three more victories in 1917, receiving the MC. He would die in action in 1918.

William Robert Gregory, only son of the Right Honourable Sir William Gregory KCMG, from Country Galway, Ireland, became an ace in 1917, but only scored four in the FE8, the first being a Roland on 4 November 1916. Robert also won the MC, plus the Légion d'Honneur and Croix de Guerre. He claimed a total of eight victories (four flying Nieuports) but died in a flying accident commanding 66 Squadron in Italy in January 1918.

Another Allied machine now in France was the Sopwith 1½ Strutter, a two-seat fighting reconnaissance machine that could also carry bombs. It was initially ordered by the RNAS, but the RFC could see its potential and also ordered some. No. 70 Squadron was the first to take the Sopwith to France, in May 1916, but it was soon evident that it had its work cut out to stay alive against a determined German. Nevertheless, the Sopwiths undertook long-range reconnaissance missions and, despite casualties, often managed to fight their way to and from an objective, provided some friendly clouds came to their aid.

On their patrols, often referred to as DOPs (Distant Offensive Patrols), No. 70 Squadron would fly deep into enemy territory to carry out their reconnaissance missions and, of course, met enemy fighters. One crew that began well was that of Second Lieutenants A. M. Vaucour and his observer, A. J. Bott. On 2 September 1916 they claimed two Fokkers, seen to go down 'out of control' and on the 14th forced another to land. The next day, during a fight, they observed two Fokkers collide, one of which fell away and was seen to crash. On 10 November, Bunny Vaucour, with another observer, forced another down, leaving a trail of smoke. Three of his claims were recorded and, in 1918, he was put in command of 45 Squadron in Italy, where he claimed four more victories. Sadly he was killed on 16 July of that year, mistakenly attacked by an Italian pilot. Vaucour had received both the MC and DFC.

Alan Bott, a former artilleryman, was likewise credited with three victories as an observer, and received the MC. In 1918 he trained as a pilot and became an ace, flying with 111 Squadron in the Middle East. He wrote the famous book *An Airman's Outings with the RFC* under the pen name of 'Contact' and later helped found Pan Books.

There were other pilots in 70 who began their careers in air fighting. One was Captain W. G. S. Sanday. On 6 September he and his observer shot down a Roland CII in flames, its crew being Willi Fahlbusch and Hans Rosencrantz of Kasta 1 who had achieved five victories by this time. William Sanday had already forced down an Albatros C-type whilst flying BE2s with No. 2 Squadron in 1915, its crew, from FA202, being taken prisoner. Three more claims with 70 Squadron, and a fifth in July 1917 flying a Spad while commanding 19 Squadron, made him an ace. He received the DSO and MC.

In truth other crews of 70 Squadron also fired at Fahlbusch's Roland, including Captain G. L. Cruickshank and his observer, Lieutenant Preston. Guy Cruickshank, born in 1890, had learned to fly in France in 1913 and was among the first RFC airmen to go to France after war was declared, flying with 3 Squadron. He flew many missions, including bombing, for which he received the MC. Soon afterwards he received the DSO for landing a spy behind the enemy's lines. On 16 September, flying over the third phase of the Battle of the Somme, he was shot down and killed by none other than Oswald Boelcke, the German's twenty-sixth victory.

Lieutenants W. J. K. Cochrane-Patrick and B. P. G. Beanlands also opened their scores with 70 Squadron. The former would achieve twenty-one victories by mid-1917, and Paul Beanlands eight by early 1918. Actually, Irish-born Cochrane-Patrick, son of Sir Noel Cochrane-Patrick, had achieved an impressive first victory before joining 70. He had been with No.1 Aircraft Depot at St Omer, as a test pilot but, on 26 April 1916, he was sent up in a Nieuport to engage a two-seater LVG. He attacked and sent it down to crash inside Allied lines, with both crewmen dead from his bullets. The LVG was from FA5 and it earned Cochrane-Patrick the Military Cross

* *

Jasta 1 began scoring against the Allies on 24 August 1916, Offizierstellvertreter Leopold Reimann downing a Sopwith two-seater of 70 Squadron. Hauptmann Martin Zander, leader of Jasta 1, shot down an FE2b on 25 August. He had already claimed two kills with Kek Nord in 1915, and perhaps even three. As related in Chapter 2, on 14 December 1915 he claimed an FB5 of 11 Squadron, piloted by Gilbert Insall VC, who became a prisoner. By the end of the year, Zander had five (probably six) victories, but by this time had retired from active duty at the front.

Gustav Leffers, of course, was now flying with Jasta 1 and, between its formation and 9 November, brought his score to nine. However, on 27 December, he was in a fight with 11 Squadron and was shot down by Captain J. B. Quested and his observer, Lieutenant H. J. H. Dicksee. It was John Quested's seventh victory. However, there was another rising star with Jasta 1 at this time, Hans von Keudell. Born in 1892, and educated in Berlin, he had been a former *uhlan*, fighting in France and Poland until he moved to aviation in June 1915. He flew two-seaters and then fighters with Kek B, with his friend Hans Bethge, and both men were now with Jasta 1.

Von Keudell would claim ten victories by the end of 1916, including a BE12 on 28 October. The BE12 was really just a BE2 with the front observer's cockpit covered over to make it a single-seater. It was something of a stop-gap attempt at increasing the RFC's fighter defence of its corps machines but, in the cold light of reality, it was still more or less a BE2! Early in the New Year von Keudell was asked to form Jasta 27 but was killed in action on 15 February. Bethge, also from Berlin, was born in 1890 and was with Keudell in the same two-seater unit and also Kek B. With Jasta 1 he claimed just three victories, but in early 1917 took command of Jasta 30 and brought his score to twenty by the spring of 1918, but was then killed in action. He had just been nominated for the *Pour le Mérite* but it had not been approved by the date of his passing, and so was not awarded.

* *

Jasta 2 had its initial batch of pilots but only one operational aeroplane at the start, and quite naturally it was Boelcke who flew it. During their wait before getting into the battle, his pilots had to sit anxiously while Boelcke racked up seven victories in the first half of September. Three of these were DH2s, so it was being amply demonstrated that these pushers were no longer a major threat. On 16 October he would bring down ace Lieutenant P. A. (Langan) Byrne for his thirty-fourth victory.

Boelcke's pilots in Jasta 2 were all bursting to get into action and it came with the arrival of new Albatros DI aircraft which the pilots collected on 16 September. Until then they only had one unarmed Albatros, a Fokker DI, a refurbished Halberstadt, and an Eindecker, all for training, plus the Fokker DIII which Boelcke used. That same evening, Otto Höhne flew over the front and shot down an FE2b. On the 17th Erwin Böhme shot down a Sopwith two-seater. Much to everyone's delight, in the late morning, the Jasta, out hunting with their leader, engaged a formation of FE2b machines of 11 Squadron and claimed three. Boelcke got one, Hans Reimann another, with the third going to Manfred von Richthofen.

For von Richthofen it was the first of a massive eighty victories he would achieve before his own death on 21 April 1918. He would be the war's ace-of-aces and received virtually every medal and award that a German aviator could have bestowed upon him.

Once unleashed, Boelcke's fledgling pilots would score heavily against the RFC on their part of the front. Looking down the roster of pilot victories, almost everyone who scored a victory in these first weeks became aces. By the end of the year its victories totalled something like eighty-five. By that date, Richthofen had scored fifteen kills, Böhme eight, Hans Imelmann six and Max Müller five. Müller, a Bavarian, born in 1887, had learned to fly in 1913. Soon after war began he broke both legs in a crash but was flying at the front by 1916, on two-seaters

Stefan Kirmaier, who had arrived with eight victories while flying with Kek Jametz, had increased this by three. Kirmaier may well have been assigned to Jasta 2 in order to relieve Boelcke who was in need of a rest and, again, German High Command was loath to risk him falling. He was too valuable. However, having achieved a total of forty victories on 26 October, he was killed in combat on the 28th.

The Jasta was in combat with DH2s of 24 Squadron but, in the whirl of a dog-fight, Erwin Böhme collided with his leader, badly smashing Boelcke's top wing. There was no chance of survival from a fall from height and perhaps the best tactical German fighting pilot of the war died as his machine hit the ground. It was a bitter blow to Jasta 2 and an even greater tragedy for Böhme. However, it did not break him and he went on to achieve twenty-four victories of his own and even command the Jasta in 1917; he died fighting on 29 November.

Jasta 4 had been formed around Kek Vaux, so when it was created in August 1916 it had several experienced pilots, such as Fritz Otto Bernert, Wilhelm Frankl and Hans Buddecke with Rudolf Berthold as its Staffelführer. The latter had six victories with Kek Vaux and made it eight by the end of 1916, just scraping in to receive the *Pour le Mérite* on 12 October. Buddecke had returned from the Middle East with seven victories with FA6 and raised this to ten on 23 September. Bernert, too, had scored a total of seven by the end of the year, while Frankl had achieved fourteen, having added five since his Kek Vaux days.

Oberleutnant Hans Berr had been given command of Jasta 5 in August 1916, with just two victories from his Fokker days with FA19. By December he had nine, and he too received the *Pour le Mérite*, on 4 December, shortly before the qualifying date changed making it now sixteen victories for this top award. Hans Karl Müller was an original pilot, having been posted in from Kek Avillers with three Fokker victories with Kasta 11 and the Kek. On 26 December he had become the first Jasta 5 pilot to score five victories but, with a total score of nine, was badly wounded on this date, and did not see further combat. His eighth victory had been achieved on 20 December, but too late for him to be recommended for the Blue Max.

Oswald Boelcke's Fokker DIII (352/16) which he used with his new command, Jasta 2, in September 1916. The days of German monoplanes were over – until 1918.

Boelcke climbing from the cockpit of an Albatros DII (386/16) at Lagnicourt in October 1916. His pilots are eager to hear about his latest flight and his latest victory. Boelcke would be killed flying this machine.

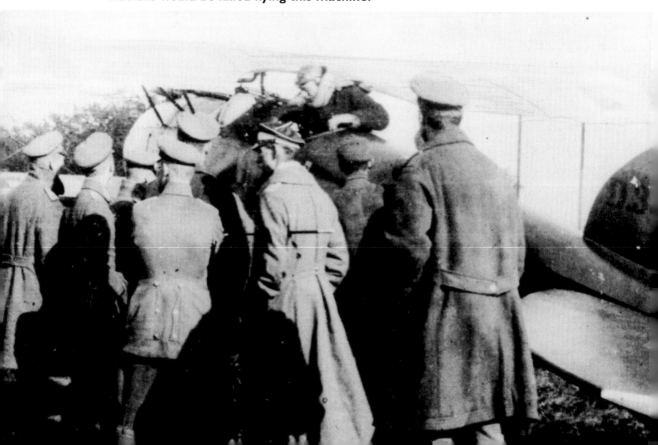

After a delay, the new aircraft for Jasta 2 arrive and stand in line. The Albatros DII was the forerunner of an Albatros design that would remain active to the end of the war; they were the DIII, DV and DVa models.

Four of Jasta 2's pilots smile for the camera. L to r: Stefan Kirmaier, who would take command of the Jasta after Boelcke's death, Hans Imelmann (six victories) (no relation to the famous Max Immelmann), Manfred von Richthofen, destined to become the highest scoring fighter ace of the war, and Hans Wortmann (two victories). The propeller is covered to protect the wood against the elements.

A wingless BE12, one of two brought down on 22 October 1916. One fell to Boelcke, his thirty-eighth victory, and one to Leopold Reimann, his fifth kill. The BE12 was a BE2 with the observer's forward cockpit covered over. The pilot had a machine gun, which can be seen by the cockpit. It was hoped that it would be an adversary for German fighters, but it remained a BE2 in all but name.

Boelcke, with hands on hips, standing with other notable air fighters shortly before his death: von Althaus (Jasta 4), Alfred Lenz (Jasta 4), Boelcke and Dielsch. The aircraft is a Halberstadt DII.

Oswald Boelcke, *Pour le Mérite*. On the left side of his tunic is the Iron Cross First Class, and pilot's badge. Through the button hole is the ribbon of the Iron Cross Second Class, under the ribbon and swords of the Royal Hohenzollern House Order.

Close friends Erwin Böhme and Oswald Boelcke. Böhme was devastated after colliding with Boelcke's Albatros on 28 October 1916, but he carried on to become a high-scoring ace himself and later commanded the Jasta

Hans von Keudell gained ten victories in 1916 flying with Jasta 1. A former *uhlan* he had fought in France and Poland before joining the air service. He would gain one more victory with Jasta 1 in January 1917 before being given command of Jasta 27. With this staffel he brought his score to twelve, but was killed in action on 15 February.

The DH2 pusher fighter, a machine that helped wrest the dominance of the Fokker Eindeckers from the skies over France in 1916.

The other pusher fighter was the FE8. This picture shows Captain F. J. Powell MC, who had one of two prototype FEs to use in 5 Squadron in early 1916. He is able to move the machine gun, but it was generally found to be better if it were fixed to fire forwards. The FE8 was slightly faster than the DH2 and eventually equipped three main scout units in France. Spare ammunition drums were carried, as with the DH2, in a container at the side of the cockpit.

Captain F. J. Powell MC became a flight commander with 40 Squadron, and is seen here with brother pilots at Aire in September 1916. Note that the gun is in a more permanently fixed position. He later commanded 41 Squadron.

A Martinsyde G102 shot down by Kurt Wintgens on 30 July 1916 for his twelfth victory. The pilot from 27 Squadron was taken prisoner.

This Martinsyde G100 was shot down on 24 September 1916, also by Kurt Wintgens, one of two claims he made that day. The machine, 27 Squadron of course, has had German markings painted over the British markings. These two victories were his eighteenth and nineteenth – and his last for he fell in flames the next day, probably shot down by Alfred Heurtaux of N3. Wintgens was still flying a Fokker Eindecker and was the French ace's eighth victory.

FE8 no.7624, marked with a '6', was from 40 Squadron. Captain T. Mapplebeck was brought down by anti-aircraft fire on 9 November 1916 and captured. However, he was also claimed by Erwin Böhme of Jasta 2 for his sixth victory.

FE8 no.7624, referred to previously, has also been remarked after its capture by the Germans, although the number '6' remains on the nacelle.

Lieutenant R. Gregory, the only son of Sir William Gregory KCMG. From Galway, Ireland, he too achieved success with FE8s in 40 Squadron. He claimed, perhaps, seven victories, but only one in 1916. He died in a crash in early 1918. His collar badge is that of the Connaught Rangers; he was commissioned in the regiment's 4th (Special Reserve) Battalion.

Lieutenant E. L. Benbow while an observer with 4 Squadron before becoming a scout pilot, flying the FE8 with 40 Squadron. He scored a total of eight victories on the type, the highest scorer on the FE8 and was awarded the MC. Five of these were scored in the final weeks of 1916. He was killed in 1918.

The Sopwith Strutter began to arrive in France in late 1916, going initially to RNAS squadrons, but the RFC began to take them on charge in 1917. As can be seen it carried a single Vickers machine gun set to fire through the propeller arc while the observer had a moveable Lewis gun for rear defence.

Major A. M. Vaucour MC and Bar DFC, as CO of 45 Squadron in 1918. The other medal ribbon beneath his wings is the Italian Silver Medal for Military Valour. He was credited with three Fokkers 'shot down' while flying with 70 Squadron, and possibly a fourth. As CO of 45 he had no need to fly combat but, out alone on 16 July 1918, his Camel was misidentified by an Italian pilot and he was killed in the attack. Vaucour was commissioned in the Royal Artillery whose collar badges he wears.

Vaucour's observer in 70 Squadron, A. J. Bott, also received the MC for his prowess as a gunner/observer. He later became a pilot and brought his score to five while flying Nieuports in the Middle East with 111 Squadron.

Max Müller was another Jasta 2 pilot and he, too, became a leading ace and was awarded the *Pour le Mérite*. In this picture we see the Iron Cross Second Class, and the Bavarian Military Merit Order, Fourth Class with Swords, hanging from his tunic button hole. The folded ribbon above his flying badge represents his Prince Regent Luitpold Medal in Bronze.

Martin Zander wearing the Iron Cross First Class, and the ribbon of the Second Class. The '9' patch on his sleeve denotes his unit at this time, FA9b. He scored three victories in 1915 with Kek Nord, and three more in 1916 while leader of Jasta 1.

William J. C. K. Cochrane-Patrick won the MC for bringing down an LVG inside Allied lines in April 1916. He was credited with two more victories with 70 Squadron and later, as a single-seat fighter pilot, brought his score to twenty-one by mid-1917, which brought him a Bar to his MC and then the DSO.

Chapter Eight
The End of 1916

As 1916 came to an end it can be said that much had changed since the war began both on the ground and in the air. From the air war's stuttering start, much had been achieved and learnt by both sides and all had needed to be understood following the establishment of the trench lines which made this modern war a static one.

Aeroplane designers had begun the race for better machines, better engines and more reliable ways of mounting machine guns onto them. The corps squadrons had honed their skills in reconnaissance, artillery spotting and photographing enemy positions. On the Allied side squadrons and escadrilles had established the same aircraft types per unit and were more or less divided between fighting units, bombing units and reconnaissance units.

On the German side they had for some time been able to dominate to a large degree the air space on their side of the lines with their Fokkers, but this had been slowly wrested from them by the Allied airmen with better fighting aeroplanes and by using the experience gained by the early aces. However, since late August 1916 the German Air Service had moved into a new era, that of the Jastas. Gone were the days of two or three fighting aeroplanes being attached to the various *flieger abteilungen*; they were now being grouped in fighting units, with experienced leaders in place. It had been envisaged that each Jasta would have around fourteen pilots on strength but, as things developed, this proved not to be the case and invariably a Jasta would have no more men on call than an RFC scout squadron would have in a flight.

Each RFC scout squadron was divided into three flights, A, B and C, each led by a flight commander, and commanded overall by a man of major's rank, although not always a man with scout experience. As the Jastas developed it soon became apparent that, within each one, a pilot of outstanding ability would emerge and that man would be the first to attack from a formation and, protected by his comrades, would make the initial kills before a general mix-up developed, allowing one or two other pilots to have a crack at the enemy.

There were a few Jastas that produced a good number of exceptional pilots, such as Jasta 2, but, as later became the case, the average Jasta had just one or two high-scoring aces backed up by other members. In 1917 the RFC and RNAS found that they were meeting larger and larger numbers of fighters, because several Jastas were grouped together, whereas the British units normally patrolled in flight sizes, usually of five machines. However, that scenario lay in the future.

❋ ❋

The pilots of the DH2 squadrons were still actively maintaining a sort of air superiority over the German side of the lines, along with the newer FE8s. The FE2b and 2d two-seaters were still making their presence felt and, despite their lumbering appearance could still see off hostile fighters, especially when fighting in a formation, sometimes a fighting circle, each gunner covering the rear end of their companions ahead of them.

Very soon the Germans began to equip wholly with the Albatros Scouts, the DII and then the DIII. The DIII was far more sleek than the DII, and was even more streamlined. Their pilots liked them, and those aces who had the ability to shoot straight and hunt in an aggressive manner soon began to have mounting scores of victories.

As already mentioned, Boelcke had fallen in October 1916 but his fledglings were proving a great problem for the RFC squadrons on the British front. On 23 November Manfred von Richthofen, in a long duel with a DH2, finally shot it down, the British pilot having to make a dash for the lines as his fuel tank began to run dry. Richthofen's opponent, who was killed, was the RFC's first ace, Lanoe Hawker VC DSO; it was the German's eleventh victory. On the 27th, Captain G. A. Parker DSO MC of 60 Squadron was shot down and killed by another Jasta 2 pilot, Werner Voss, his first victory, one of two he claimed that day. Voss would eventually score forty-eight victories before being killed in action in September 1917.

Captain J. D. Latta, from Willesden, London, born in 1897, flew Nieuports with 1 Squadron in 1916 gaining three victories, including two balloons. Then, with 60 Squadron, he made it five by September. Sidney Cowan, having scored six victories with 24 Squadron, joined 29 Squadron as a flight commander, downing his seventh on 17 November, but then collided with another British machine and fell to his death. He was among the first to receive the MC and two Bars, and was only 19 years of age.

One successful FE2 pilot was S. W. Price of 11 Squadron. He usually flew with an American volunteer observer, Fred Libby from Sterling, Colorado, born in 1898. Stephen Price and Libby accounted for seven enemy machines, although they were mostly the 'out of control' kind. Price was awarded the MC, and so was Libby, who later became a pilot. Noel W. W. Webb flew FEs with 25 Squadron and shot down a Fokker along with his observer, J. A. Mann. Their opponent was Otto Dappert of FA18 who lost a wing as he went down. By September Webb had five victories, and would go on to gain fourteen with 70 Squadron (Camels) until he too was downed, by Werner Voss in August 1917. Mann scored another three flying with G. R. M. Reid, who had scored nine victories by October 1916.

Maximillian John Jules Gabriel Mare-Montembault was a DH2 pilot with 32 Squadron. He scored five victories in 1916, and a sixth in early 1917, before being shot down by a future German ace, Adolf von Tutschek, the German's first victory.

John Bowley Quested flew as an observer with 11 Squadron in 1915 but then trained to be a pilot and, having done so, returned to 11 in July 1916. With his various observers he accounted for seven German aircraft that same year, plus one more in January 1917. At one stage it was thought he had shot down von Richthofen but this proved incorrect, although he did shoot down Gustav Leffers on 27 December 1916. Quested and his observer were then brought down themselves, by Wilhelm Cymera of Jasta 1, but were over the British side, and so survived. Quested received the MC and French Croix de Guerre.

Another interesting airman at the front in 1916 was Harold Evans Hartney. Canadian-born Hartney (1888) served in the Canadian Army prior to joining the RFC, going to 20 Squadron where he claimed three Fokkers, two Eindeckers on 1 July and possibly a D-model on 20 October. In February 1917 he doubled this score before being wounded. While away from the front he became a naturalised American, which led to him transferring to the US Air Service. He gained one further victory in 1918 with the 27th Aero Squadron, and ended up commanding the US 1st Pursuit Group.

John Ingles Gilmour of 27 Squadron became the highest scorer with the Martinsyde Elephant in 1916, with three victories, although he went on to claim thirty-nine by mid-1918. Ginger Gilmour from Helensborough, Scotland, transferred to the RFC from the Argyll and Sutherland Highlanders, and received the MC with 27 Squadron, although mainly for bombing trips. His later success came as a Sopwith Camel pilot.

On the French front, 1916 had seen the introduction of a new fighter, the Spad VII. Initially it carried one and then two machine guns set to fire through the propeller. In due course the Spads replaced the Nieuport Scouts, but it took some while for Escadrille designations to change, so that while, for instance, N3 had some Spads, it was some time before it changed to Spa3. The RFC saw its potential too, and eventually it equipped two fighter squadrons, 23 changing from FE2s and 19 from BE12s.

The French were also altering their fighting structure, forming a number of fighter escadrilles into Groupes de Combat. For example, N3, N26, N73 and N103 became Groupe de Combat 12 (GC12), commanded by Félix Brocard, which began operations from Cachy on 1 November, a base at the southern end of the British front. Each escadrille had its aircraft marked with a stork emblem, although each in different poses, and collectively they became *The Storks* Group.

Georges Guynemer, now flying Spads, scored his nineteenth victory on 10 November 1916, by downing a Jasta 6 machine in flames and followed this with an Albatros C from FA59. The Frenchman made it twenty-three by shooting down a pilot of Jasta 12 on the 22nd, shortly after bagging a Halberstadt C-type. Just after Christmas he brought his score to twenty-five, an Albatros C of KG4.

Nungesser downed a machine from KG5 on 23 November, then scored three times in December, a Halberstadt and an LVG on the 4th and a fighter on the 20th (plus a probable), to make his 1916 total twenty-eight. The Halberstadt was from FA22, crewed by Hans Schilling and pilot Leutnant Rosenbachs, Schilling being killed. This successful German observer had been teamed up with Albert Dossenbach and had shot down nine Allied aircraft during the year but had been shot down themselves on 27 September. This ninth victory had been an FE2b of 25 Squadron, its crew being V. W. Harrison and Sergeant L. S. Court, but they came down on the British side, Schilling on the German. Les Court received the French Médaille Militaire and went on to achieve eight victories by the end of 1916.

Albert Dossenbach had won both classes of the Iron Cross early in the war as a lance corporal with the medical service, once carrying his wounded CO out of the range of enemy fire. Transferring to aviation he trained as a pilot and joined FA22 in June 1916. After their eight victories, and recovering from burns after his shoot-down, Dossenbach teamed up with another observer and gained a ninth victory on 3 November. A week later he received the *Pour le Mérite*, the first two-seater pilot so honoured, and the last but one (Berr) to be awarded the Blue Max after eight victories. Later he became a single-seat pilot, bringing his personal score to fifteen before he himself was killed in action in 1917.

Stefan Kirmaier, leader of Jasta 2, lost his life on 22 November in a fight with DH2s of 24 Squadron. He was shot down by J. O. Andrews, born in Waterloo, Lancashire, who had earlier served with the Royal Scots. It was his seventh victory since July, and five of these had been fighters. Andrews would eventually achieve twelve victories by mid-1917, having moved to 66 Squadron, flying Sopwith Pups, and winning the DSO, MC and Bar.

Selden Herbert Long was another successful DH2 pilot with 24 Squadron. From Aldershot, born in 1895, he came from the Durham Light Infantry, and was known as 'Tubby'. His first victory was a Fokker 'out of control' on 6 August, then a Roland on 16 November. In December he claimed four more and, in early 1917, brought his total to nine, and also won the DSO and MC. Yarmouth-born Eric Pashley, who had lived in London before the war, learned to fly in 1911 and as war came he flew as a test pilot. In late 1916 he managed a posting to 24 Squadron and in the final weeks of the year downed five German machines, then another three in early 1917, including two of Jasta 2's pilots. Pashley was recommended for the MC, but before it was confirmed he was killed in action on 17 March 1917.

Hans Karl Müller, of Jasta 5, fell on 26 December. This 24-year old from Saxony had earlier flown with FA3, then Kek Avillers. On the 26th he had shot down a BE2c for his ninth victory, but was hit in the abdomen and seriously wounded. He saw no further combat. He had attacked a machine from 9 Squadron flown by R. W. P. Hall and E. F. W. Smith, with the Halberstadt just ninety feet away. The British crew watched as it staggered and went down to crash.

On the 27th French fighter ace Pierre Augustin Francois Violet-Marty was shot down in flames over Ornes. He had been in the artillery but moved to aviation soon after the war began. His first escadrille was MF55, with which he won the Military Medal but, requesting fighters, was moved to N57. Between 6 October, when he downed a Fokker, and his death, he achieved five victories and three probables.

There is no information about his loss, so perhaps the observer in the Aviatik he was in the process of shooting down also shot down his Nieuport 17.

The year 1916 had been a trying one for the air forces of both sides. The Fokker monoplanes had been defeated, the DH2s and FE8s were soon to be outclassed by the new, sleek, German D-types, especially the Albatros, and the Germans were also establishing their Jagdstaffeln. At least both sides now had interrupter gears for their mounted machine guns, and a vast amount of experience had been gained by air fighters on both sides of the lines. 1917 would see many more developments in this First Air War.

Major L. G. Hawker VC DSO, the RFC's first ace. Commanding 24 Squadron in 1916, he was shot down and killed by Manfred von Richthofen on 9 November, the Baron's eleventh victory.

Pilots of Jasta 2 soon after Boelcke had fallen. L to r: Jürgen Sandel, Max Müller, Manfred von Richthofen, Wolfgang Günther, Hans Kirmaier, Hans Imelmann, Erich König, Otto Höhne, Hans Wortmann and Dieter Collin.

J. D. Latta MC flew with 60 Squadron, claiming two victories. This made it five when added to three claims he made while with 1 Squadron in June 1916, two of them being over kite balloons. He became a prisoner of war in 1917.

Captain S. W. Price MC, an FE2b pilot with 11 Squadron in 1916. He scored seven victories between August and October, six of them with his American observer, Fred Libby, who also received the MC.

Fred Libby flew as an observer with 11 Squadron in 1916 and shared six victories with his pilot, Stephen Price, both being awarded the MC. Libby was a cowboy from Colorado and had previously been an observer in 23 Squadron. With a total of ten victories he became a pilot, flying with 43 Squadron and 25 Squadron in 1917 bringing his score to fourteen. After this he transferred to the US Air Service.

N. W. W. Webb MC claimed five victories as an FE2b pilot with 25 Squadron in 1916, winning the MC. He later flew Sopwith Camels with 70 Squadron but was killed in action in 1917 after a total of fourteen victories. Webb's first victory on 19 July was in company with observer J. A. Mann; a Fokker from FA18.

One of Webb's observers in 25 Squadron, J. A. Mann MC, scored one victory. He then flew with G. R. M. Reid, claiming three more kills. On 9 August he and another pilot were shot down in flames.

G. R. M. Reid flew with 25 Squadron in 1916, scoring three victories in May for which he received the MC. He then moved to 20 Squadron as a flight commander, with FE2d machines, adding six more victories to his tally, including two Fokker DIIs, which brought him a Bar to his MC. He later commanded a bombing squadron and at the end of the war was awarded the DSO. He retired as Air Vice Marshal Sir Ranold Reid KCB.

DH2 pilots of 32 Squadron in 1916. L to r: W. G. S. Curphey MC & Bar, Henty, F. H. Coleman, M. J. J. G. Mare-Montembault and R. E. Wilson. Curphey gained three victories in 1916 and three more in early 1917. Mare-Montembault claimed five in 1916 and one more in 1917. On 10 October he was shot down by Oswald Boelcke, the German's thirty-fourth victory, but survived. Wilson was also shot down by Boelcke, victory number twenty, on 2 September, but he became a prisoner.

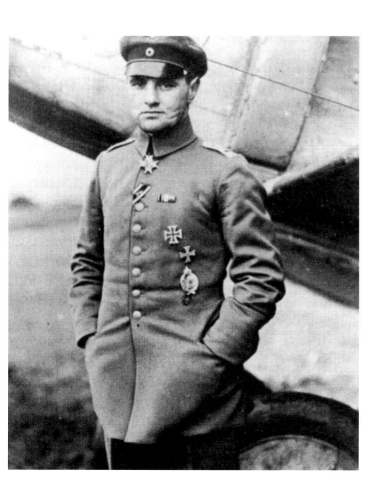

Albert Dossenbach was the first German two-seater pilot to be awarded the Blue Max, on 11 November 1916. Flying with FA22 he and his observer accounted for nine Allied aircraft. Going over to single-seaters he brought his score to fifteen by mid-1917, having just taken command of Jasta 10. He was shot down and killed attacking a DH4 bomber on 3 July 1917.

A 12 Squadron BE2c brought down by Stefan Kirmaier on 21 October 1916, his fifth victory. Its pilot, A. B. Raymond-Barker, was wounded and taken prisoner. His brother, Major Richard Raymond-Barker MC, became an ace on Bristol Fighters in 1917 and, in September 1917, took command of 3 Squadron flying Camels. On 20 April 1918 he became the seventy-ninth victory of Manfred von Richthofen, who had been under Kirmaier in 1916.

Stefan Kirmaier took over Jasta 2 after Boelcke's death (the Jasta became known as Jasta Boelcke), but having achieved eleven victories fell in combat with DH2s of 24 Squadron on 22 November.

Captain J. O. Andrews of 24 Squadron was the pilot who downed Kirmaier – his seventh victory. He claimed five more in 1917 with 66 Squadron, receiving the DSO and MC.

Another successful DH2 pilot with 24 Squadron was Captain S. H. Long, whose combat successes also brought him the DSO and MC. Selden Long claimed six victories with the DH2 in 1916 and three more in 1917.

J. B. Quested flew FE2b pushers with 11 Squadron in 1916, being awarded the MC and French Croix de Guerre. With his various observers he claimed seven of his eight victories in 1916, one being the German ace Gustav Leffers on 27 December; Leffers was flying an Albatros DI. Leffers was a nine-victory ace and occasionally flew a captured Nieuport Scout with German markings. There is a suggestion that Leffers was flying this machine when he died.

John I. Gilmour ended the war with the DSO, MC and two Bars, and a victory score of thirty-nine. His first three, one Albatros D and two Fokkers, were claimed whilst flying a Martinsyde G100 in September 1916. His main success, however, was as a Sopwith Camel pilot in the first half of 1918.

H. E. Hartney was born in Canada and joined the RFC, flying FE2s with 20 Squadron. In 1916 he and his observers shot down three Fokkers 'out of control'. In 1917 he claimed three more D-type fighters. He later became an American citizen and served with the US Air Service, commanding a squadron and then a pursuit group. He is seen here in the uniform of the USAS in 1918, wearing the US pilot's wings; his first medal ribbon is the US DSC.

A good shot of the front gunner/observer in an **FE2d**. Invariably the man had to stand up in his cockpit in order to operate his gun, and always to operate the rear-firing gun, fixed on a mounting at the rear of the cockpit and set to fire back over the top wing. The bag underneath the gun was to collect spent shells so that they didn't fall into the nacelle and foul the pilot's controls.

This captured **FE2d** (the 'd' model is identified by having a radiator behind the pilot's cockpit). In the foreground is the front gun, which has been taken from its position, some ammunition drums and bombs. The rear-firing gun and mounting can clearly be seen. The forward skid is to aid landing, preventing the machine nosing over.

The Albatros DII of Jasta 2, flown by Karl Büttner, shot down and captured on 16 November 1916. He was brought down by the BE2 crew from 8 Squadron of Captain G. A. Parker and H. E. Hervey. It was the first Albatros DII brought down in Allied lines, and both men received the MC for this achievement. Parker, of course, was later shot down by Voss.

Captain G. A. Parker DSO MC of 60 Squadron. Voss shot him down on 27 November 1916, the German's first of forty-eight victories. The photograph has been doctored to show the ribbons of his decorations; his Army insignia is that of the Northamptonshire Regiment. An observer before becoming a pilot, he flew with 6 Squadron. In March 1916, now a pilot, he joined 13 Squadron before going to 8 Squadron and then 60 Squadron later that year.

Werner Voss was destined to be a well-known German ace. He claimed his first victim with Jasta 2 on 27 November 1916, shooting down Captain G.A. Parker DSO MC.

Büttner's Albatros DII was the first captured German machine to be designated by the RFC with a 'G' number (G for German), a system which began in November 1916, and so it became G1. Its German markings have been over-painted and the British roundel, plus red, white and blue tail stripes applied. The German's personal marking of Bü remains.

A Nieuport 17 of Escadrille N77, brought down by Hermann Kunz of Jasta 7 on 23 October 1916. It was the German's first victory and also the first victory of his Jasta. Kunz claimed another Nieuport on 11 November, but did not score again until October 1917. He ended the war with six victories, his last three whilst operating in Palestine.

A Spad VII flown by Georges Guynemer in Spa3. The Spad had started arriving in French escadrilles during 1916 and was soon the main fighter aeroplane used by the French Air Service. Note the familiar name *Vieux Charles* on the fuselage, and the Spa3 stork marking. The aeroplane in the background is a British Sopwith Triplane of the RNAS.

Cyril Pashley of 24 Squadron in 1916-17 claimed eight victories in the DH2. He had learned to fly in September 1911 at the age of 19. He was killed in action on 17 March 1917.